C000133509

on
death

John Donne
on
death

ET REMOTISSIMA PROPE

'on'

'on'
Published by Hesperus Press Limited
4 Rickett Street, London sw6 1RU
www.hesperuspress.com

First published 1632–40
First published by Hesperus Press Limited, 2008

Foreword © Edward Docx, 2008

Designed and typeset by Fraser Muggeridge studio
Printed in Jordan by Jordan National Press

ISBN: 978-1-84391-600-0

All rights reserved. This book is sold subject to the condition that it shall not
be resold, lent, hired out or otherwise circulated without the express prior
consent of the publisher.

Contents

Foreword

On picking up this book, two questions will no doubt present themselves more or less immediately: why John Donne and why John Donne on death?

The first is less difficult to answer: to my mind John Donne (1572–1631) is the most interesting English poet of whom we have any decent record. Artistically, he is almost unique in his ability to render the action of the mind, body and spirit with equal fidelity in a single work – sometimes, indeed, in a single line. His reputation is founded, of course, on his poetry and there we find the verse vividly alive with the astonishing energy of his character: he is libertine, supplicant, mourner and sensualist by turn; the heartless rejecter *and* the heartbroken lover; the tender companion and the scornful enemy; the jocular rake, the consoling admirer, the lawyerly counsellor; both egotist and reticent. But in the sermons, though an older man living in dramatically different circumstances, Donne's startling animus is still present. He remains wrathful, artful, generous, vicious, brilliant, too clever for his own good; elegant, concise, ingenious, long-winded, crude, disgusting, paradoxical, morbid, supremely original and supremely inventive. More than all of this, he retains his breathtaking facility with our language and some of the lines he writes are both exquisite and eternal. Indeed, it is something of an eye-opener for many people (myself included) when they learn that his two most famous lines – 'no man is an island' and 'never send to know for whom the bell tolls; it tolls for thee'[*] – are not taken from *The Songs and Sonnets* of his younger days but the later period of the sermons when Donne was well into his fifties and a man of the cloth.

So much for his art. But what of the life? As ever the two are intimately related – and it is no coincidence that the great

[*] 'Meditation 17', 1624.

stylistic master of antithesis lived in the most compellingly antithetical age of our history. At its manly noon, England swarmed with spies, significant and petty; plots and counter plots were hatched, foiled and revisited; ruin was a whim and fortune a favour. Remember, this was the time when the Churches of Rome and of England were at one another's throats, without let or very much mercy, through reign after reign after reign. Parliament was a wasps' nest of intrigue, rivalled only by the bear's pit of the court and the weasel-warrens of clergydom – all of which institutions intrigued against each other constantly. Everything was political (including and most of all religion), and everything was religious (including and most of all politics). There was actual war, the constant threat of war, or someone trying to stir up one of the two. Meanwhile, men were tortured and murdered, casually, regularly. And pretty much everyone, from monarch to manservant, was required to contend with the endless resentments and factionalism and rivalry and blood that such circumstances engendered.

Donne lived busily in the dangerous thick of all this and his life provides us with a spellbinding commentary. In his sixty odd years, he journeyed from the committed-though-covert Catholic family circumstances of his boyhood to become the most celebrated protestant preacher of the times, the Dean of St Paul's. He converted himself from the devil-may-care philandering poet of his youthful verse to the conscientious, God-fearing, forensic theologian of his sermons. He was lawyer, soldier, secretary, social pariah and parish pillar. He saw it all. And he adjusted and accommodated himself, sometimes year by year, to what he saw.

In short, though the poetry of the younger Donne will always be his principal legacy, it is only in the sermons of his old age that we can enjoy the full and fierce convening of *all* of that life and *all* of those times. Here you find Donne attempting to account for and synthesise the contortions, contradictions and conflicts that raged about him and that burned within. This is the voice of the wiser man, deeper and more seasoned, a survivor, a veteran of life and death.

Which brings us to our second question: why Donne on Death? The answer here takes us into territory less widely known. But to put it baldly: there can be no other front rank writer in the English language who has thought, written and talked about the subject more. And once again, Donne has every angle covered – intellectual, spiritual, physical (those three again). If Love was the boon companion-adversary of Donne's youth, then Death was no less the intimate of his old age.

The reasons for this familiarity are legion but, for the sake of brevity, they are to do on the one side with the extraordinary amount of death that Donne himself personally lived through, and on the other with the nature of his particular struggle with his faith, his God, and more specifically his own personal salvation. Or lack of it.

A quick inventory of the people Donne lost before he himself died reveals his personal sufferings at Death's hand: his father, when he was four, three of his sisters by the time he was ten, his brother when a young man, his wife, at least eight of his own children (including still births), his best friends, male and female, his favourite correspondents, not to mention dozens of others with whom he was cordial. Then, right at the end, his mother. In addition, during his later years, the plague returned and ravaged London like no time since the Black Death – in 1625 people were dying at the rate of 4000 *a week*. It is also worth noting that Donne himself thought he was several times going to pass away from his various sicknesses, fevers and ailments: 'I think Death will play with me so long, as he will forget to kill me', he wrote to Mrs Cockayne, one of his close correspondents in later years. Moreover, on more than one occasion, several people in and around the court assumed he actually was dead and various informal obituaries began to appear.

Donne's intimate friend-and-foe attitude to Death is perhaps best illustrated by an extraordinary 'Death be not proud'[*] piece of theatre he himself orchestrated in the last weeks of his life. Knowing full well that the bell was greatly overdue for tolling, he carefully assembled various props – a wooden platform cut in the shape of a funeral urn, a shroud, a life-size board – and had a final likeness of himself drawn. And very scary it is too: a withered, wizened, emaciated old man stares out from the hooded folds 'with so much of the sheet turned aside as might shew his lean, pale and death-like face', as Izaak Walton, Donne's first biographer wrote in 1639. Stranger and more macabre yet, he so loved the portrait that he had it placed beside his bed. To all intents and purposes, for the last few days of his life, John Donne slept with his own death's-head.

This real and ongoing experience of death is nowhere better illustrated than in *Death's Duel* – collected here. This was Donne's last public oration and it is an extraordinary piece of work if for no other reason than that it is totally and utterly saturated in death, the central thesis being that everything that happens to a human being – everything – is at root a preparation for, or a premonition of, Death. Listen to this, for example, where he manages to make even the *womb* a presage; remember, too, that shroud of his death's-head portrait, and the fact that Donne's mother has recently died:

> We have a winding sheet in our mother's womb which grows with us from our conception, and we come into the world wound up in that winding sheet, for we come to seek a grave… we celebrate our own funerals with cries even at our birth; as though our threescore and ten years of life were spent in our mother's labour, and our circle made up in the first point thereof… And we come into a world that lasts many ages, but we last not.

[*] 'Holy Sonnet X'.

Even when considering the other side of Donne's struggle with death – the less corporeal, more theological side – it is important to keep in mind that the concepts of heaven and salvation were not to Donne concepts at all, but twin realities. Twin realities that he lived in genuine fear of not attaining. It is not that much of an exaggeration to say that the Donne you will find in these sermons was, from time to time, absolutely terrified that the licentious braggart of his younger days would never be forgiven. Worse still, as a Protestant minister, he could no longer even shoot for purgatory. Or at least not officially. In these lines from the 1629 sermon (also collected here), you can hear him talking to his congregation; but what gives the address that extra energy and dramatic power, I think, is that you can also hear him talking to himself:

> Therefore to that mistaking soul, that discomposed, that shivered and shrivelled and ravelled and ruined soul, to that jealous and suspicious soul only, I say with the Apostle, *Let no man judge you*, intruding into those things which he hath not seen. Let no man make you afraid of secret purposes in God... The law alone were much too heavy if there were not a superabundant ease and alleviation in that hand that Christ Jesus reaches out to us.

In truth, many of the passages in these sermons sound as much like prayers as preaching.

Thus the reasons to study Donne, and Donne on Death in particular. But one more thing needs to be pointed up before we take the plunge: that these sermons are primarily *performances* not essays; and that a sermon is a very particular form of drama – full of rhetoric and gesture, exhortation and refutation. A sermon lives when it is heard and seen – even if only in the imagination.

Perhaps it will be helpful, therefore, to imagine yourself in his congregation, and to conjure up Donne himself, speaking aloud, standing up there in the pulpit, arrayed in his holy vestments.

Remember, too, that Donne was conscious of his own appearance – especially by the time of *Death's Duel* – and that this was also part of the theatre.

You have before you a cadaverous man of long fame and varied reputation, a grey bearded veteran of three monarchs, ferociously intelligent, eloquent and impassioned, though well informed and scholarly withal. While all around you sit the most important people in England, many of whom have come especially to hear him, often times including the King. And be in no doubt; though he faces some formidable competition for the crown of the greatest poet of his age, John Donne bows to no one when it comes to sermons.

– Edward Docx, 2008

On Death

An Easter Sermon

28th March 1619

*Preached to the Lords upon Easter Day, at the Communion,
the King being then dangerously sick at Newmarket.*

> What man is he that liveth, and shall not see death?
> Psalm 89:48

At first, God gave the judgement of death upon man, when he
should transgress, absolutely, *Morte morieris*, Thou shalt surely
die. The woman in her dialogue with the Serpent, she mol-
lifies it, *Ne fortè moriamur*, Perchance, if we eat, we may die; and
then the Devil is as peremptory on the other side, *Nequaquam
moriemini*, Do what you will, surely you shall not die. And now
God in this text comes to his reply, *Quis est homo*, shall they not
die? Give me but one instance, but one exception to this rule,
What man is he that liveth, and shall not see death? Let no man, no
woman, no devil offer a *Ne fortè* (perchance we may die), much
less a *Nequaquam* (surely we shall not die), except he be provided
of an answer to this question, except he can give an instance
against this general, except he can produce that man's name,
and history, that hath lived, and shall not see death. We are all
conceived in close prison; in our mothers' wombs, we are close
prisoners all; when we are born, we are born but to the liberty of
the house, prisoners still, though within larger walls; and then
all our life is but a going out to the place of execution, to death.
Now was there ever any man seen to sleep in the cart, between
Newgate, and Tyburn? Between the prison, and the place of
execution, does any man sleep? And we sleep all the way; from
the womb to the grave we are never thoroughly awake; but pass
on with such dreams and imaginations as these: I may live as
well as another, and why should I die, rather than another? But

awake, and tell me, says this text, *Quis homo?* Who is that other that thou talkest of? *What man is he that liveth, and shall not see death?*

In these words, we shall first, for our general humiliation, consider the unanswerableness of this question, There is no man that lives, and shall not see death. Secondly, we shall see how that modification of Eve may stand, *fortè moriemur*, how there may be a probable answer made to this question, that it is like enough that there are some men that live, and shall not see death. And thirdly, we shall find that truly spoken which the Devil spake deceitfully then, we shall find the *Nequaquam* verified, we shall find a direct and full answer to this question; we shall find a man that lives and shall not see death, our Lord and Saviour Christ Jesus, of whom both St Augustine and St Jerome do take this question to be principally asked, and this text to be principally intended. Ask me this question then, of all the sons of men, generally guilty of original sin, *Quis homo*, and I am speechless, I can make no answer. Ask me this question of those men which shall be alive upon earth at the last day, when Christ comes to judgement, *Quis homo*, and I can make a probable answer: *fortè moriemur*, perchance they shall die. It is a problematical matter, and we say nothing too peremptorily. Ask me this question without relation to original sin, *Quis homo*, and then I will answer directly, fully, confidently, *Ecce homo*, there was a man that lived and was not subject to death by the law, neither did he actually die so, but that he fulfilled the rest of this verse: *Eruit animam de inferno*, by his own power, he delivered his soul from the hand of the grave. From the first, this lesson rises, general doctrines must be generally delivered: All men must die. From the second, this lesson, collateral and unrevealed doctrines must be soberly delivered: How shall we be changed at the last day, we know not so clearly. From the third, this lesson arises, conditional doctrines must be conditionally delivered: If we be dead with him, we shall be raised with him.

4

First then, for the generality. Those other degrees of punishment which God inflicted upon Adam, and Eve, and in them upon us, were as absolutely and unlimitedly pronounced as this of death, and yet we see they are many ways extended or contracted. To man it was said, *In sudore vultus*, In the sweat of thy brows, thou shalt eat thy bread, and how many men never sweat, till they sweat with eating? To the woman it was said, Thy desire shall be to thy husband, and he shall rule over thee, and how many women have no desire to their husbands, how many overrule them? Hunger and thirst and weariness and sickness are denounced upon all, and yet if you ask me *Quis homo?* What is the man that hungers and thirsts not, that labours not, that sickens not? I can tell you of many that never felt any of these. But contract the question to that one of death, *Quis homo?* What man is he that shall not taste death? And I know none. Whether we consider the summer solstice, when the day is sixteen hours, and the night but eight, or the winter solstice, when the night is sixteen hours, and the day but eight, still all is but twenty-four hours, and still the evening and the morning make but a day. The Patriarchs in the Old Testament had their summer day, long lives; we are in the winter, short lived; but *Quis homo?* Which of them or us come not to our night in death? If we consider violent deaths, casual deaths, it is almost a scornful thing to see, with what wantonness and sportfulness, death plays with us. We have seen a man cannon-proof in the time of war, and slain with his own pistol in the time of peace. We have seen a man recovered after his drowning, and live to hang himself. But for that one kind of death, which is general (though nothing be in truth more against nature than dissolution, and corruption, which is death), we are come to call that death natural death, than which, indeed, nothing is more unnatural. The generality makes it natural. Moses says that man's age is seventy, and eighty is labour and pain; and yet himself was more than eighty, and in a good state, and habitude when he said so. No length, no strength enables us to answer this *Quis homo?* What man? &c.

5

Take a flat map, a globe *in plano*, and here is East, and there is West, as far asunder as two points can be put; but reduce this flat map to roundness, which is the true form, and then East and West touch one another, and are all one. So consider man's life aright to be a circle, *Pulvis es, & in pulverem reverteris*, Dust thou art, and to dust thou must return; *Nudus egressus, Nudus revertar*, Naked I came, and naked I must go. In this, the circle, the two points meet, the womb and the grave are but one point, they make but one station, there is but a step from that to this. This brought in that custom amongst the Greek emperors that ever at the day of their coronation, they were presented with several sorts of marble, that they might then bespeak their tomb. And this brought in that custom into the Primitive Church that they called the Martyrs' days, wherein they suffered, *Natalitia Martyrum*, their birth days; birth and death is all one.

Their death was a birth to them into another life, into the glory of God. It ended one circle, and created another; for immortality, and eternity is a circle too: not a circle where two points meet, but a circle made at once. This life is a circle, made with a compass that passes from point to point. That life is a circle stamped with a print, an endless and perfect circle, as soon as it begins. Of this circle, the mathematician is our great and good God. The other circle we make up ourselves; we bring the cradle and grave together by a course of nature. Every man does; *Mi Gheber*, says the Original. It is not Ishe, which is the first name of man in the Scriptures, and signifies nothing but a sound, a voice, a word. A musical air dies and evaporates; what wonder if man that is but Ishe, a sound, die too? It is not Adam, which is another name of man, and signifies nothing but red earth. Let it be earth red with blood (with that murder which we have done upon ourselves) let it be earth red with blushing (so the word is used in the Original), with a conscience of our own infirmity, what wonder if man that is but Adam, guilty of this self-murder in himself, guilty of this inborn frailty in himself, die too? It is not Enos, which is also a third name of man, and signifies nothing but a wretched and miserable creature; what wonder if man, that is but earth, that is a burden to his neighbours, to his friends, to his kindred, to himself, to whom all others, and to whom himself desires death, what wonder if he die? But this question is framed upon none of these names, not Ishe, not Adam, not Enos; but it is *Mi Gheber, Quis vir*, which is the word always signifying a man accomplished in all excellencies, a man accompanied with all advantages. Fame, and good opinion justly conceived, keeps him from being Ishe, a mere sound, standing only upon popular acclamation; innocence and integrity keeps him from being Adam, red earth, from bleeding, or blushing at anything he has done. That holy and religious art of arts, which St Paul professed, That he knew how to want, and how to abound, keeps him from being Enos, miserable or wretched in any fortune. He is Gheber, a great man and a good man, a happy man and a holy man, and yet *Mi Gheber, Quis homo*, this man must see death.

And therefore we will carry this question a little higher, from *Quis homo* to *Quis deorum*, Which of the gods have not seen death? Ask it of those who are gods by participation of God's power, of those of whom God says, *Ego dixi, dii estis*, and God answers for them and of them and to them, You shall die like men. Ask it of those gods who are gods by imputation, whom creatures have created, whom men have made gods, the gods of the heathen, and do we not know where all these gods died? Sometimes diverse places dispute who has their tombs; but do not they deny their godhead in confessing their tombs? Do they not all answer that they cannot answer this text, *Mi Gheber, Quis homo*, What man, *Quis deorum*, What god of man's making has not seen death? As Justin Martyr asks that question, Why should I pray to Apollo or Asclepius for health, *Qui apud Chironem medicinam didicerunt,*[1] when I know who taught them all that they knew? So why should I look for immortality from such or such a god, whose grave I find for a witness that he himself is

7

dead? Nay, carry this question higher than so, from this *Quis homo* to *quid homo*, what is there in the nature and essence of man, free from death? The whole man is not, for the dissolution of body and soul is death. The body is not; I shall as soon find an immortal rose, an eternal flower, as an immortal body. And for the immortality of the soul, it is safer said to be immortal by preservation, than immortal by nature. That God keeps it from dying, then, that it cannot die. We magnify God in a humble and faithful acknowledgement of the immortality of our souls, but if we ask, *quid homo*, what is there in the nature of man that should keep him from death, even in that point the question is not easily answered.

It is every man's case then; every man dies; and though it may perchance be but a mere Hebraism to say that every man shall see death, perchance it amounts to no more but to that phrase, *Gustare mortem*, To taste death, yet thus much may be implied in it too: that as every man must die, so every man may see that he must die; as it cannot be avoided, so it may be understood. A beast dies, but he does not see death. St Basil says he saw an ox weep for the death of his yoke-fellow, but St Basil might mistake the occasion of that ox's tears. Many men die too, and yet do not see death. The approaches of death amaze them, and stupefy them. They feel no colluctation with powers and principalities upon their death bed; that is true. They feel no terrors in their consciences, no apprehensions of judgement, upon their death bed; that is true; and this we call going away like a lamb. But the Lamb of God had a sorrowful sense of death; His soul was heavy unto death, and he had an apprehension, that his Father had forsaken him; And in this text, the Chaldee Paraphrase[2] expresses it thus: *Videbit Angelum mortis*, he shall see a messenger, a forerunner, a power of death, an executioner of death, he shall see something with horror, though not such as shall shake his moral or his Christian constancy.

So that this *Videbunt*, They shall see, implies also a *Viderunt*, They have seen, that is, they have used to see death, to observe

8

a death in the decay of themselves, and of every creature, and of the whole world. Almost fourteen hundred years ago, St Cyprian writing against Demetrianus, who imputed all the wars and deaths and unseasonablenesses of that time to the contempt and irreligion of the Christians, that they were the cause of all those ills, because they would not worship their gods, Cyprian imputes all those distempers to the age of the whole world; *Canos videmus in pueris*, says he, We see children born grey-headed. *Capilli deficiunt, antequam crescant*, Their hair is changed, before it be grown. *Nec aetas in senectute desinit, sed incipit a senectute*, We do not die with age, but we are born old. Many of us have seen death in our particular selves, in many of those steps in which the moral man expresses it. We have seen *Mortem infantiae, pueritiam*, the death of infancy in youth; and *Pueritiae, adolescentiam*, and the death of youth in our middle age. And at last we shall see *Mortem senectutis, mortem ipsam*, the death of age in death itself. But yet after that, a step farther than that moral man went, *Mortem mortis in morte Iesu*, We shall see the death of Death itself in the death of Christ. As we could not be clothed at first, in Paradise, till some Creatures were dead (for we were clothed in beasts skins), so we cannot be clothed in Heaven, but in his garment who died for us.

This *Videbunt*, this future sight of Death, implies a *viderunt*, they have seen, they have studied death in every book, in every creature; and it implies a *Vident*, they do presently see death in every object, they see the hour-glass running to the death of the hour; they see the death of some profane thoughts in themselves, by the entrance of some religious thought of compunction, and conversion to God, and then they see the death of that religious thought by an inundation of new profane thoughts that overflow those. As Christ says, that as often as we eat the sacramental bread we should remember his death, so as often as we eat ordinary bread, we may remember our death; for even hunger and thirst are diseases: they are *Mors quotidiana*, a daily death, and if they lasted long would kill us. In every object and subject, we all have and do and shall see death; not to our comfort as an end of misery, not only as such a misery in itself as the philosopher takes it to be, *Mors omnium miseriarum*, That death is the death of all misery, because it destroys and dissolves our being; but as it is *Stipendium peccati*, The reward of sin. That as Solomon says, *Indignatio Regis nuncius mortis*, The wrath of the King is as a messenger of Death, so *Mors nuncius indignationis Regis*, We see in death a testimony that our Heavenly King is angry; for, but for his indignation against our sins, we should not die. And this death, as it is *Malum*, ill (for if ye weigh it in the philosopher's balance, it is an annihilation of our present being, and if ye weigh it in the divine balance, it is a seal of God's anger against sin), so this death is general; of this, this question there is no answer, *Quis homo*, What man, &c.

We pass then from the *Morte moriemini* to the *fortè moriemini*, from the generality and the inescapableness of death, from this question, as it admits no answer, to the *Forte moriemini*, perchance we shall die; that is, to the question as it may admit a probable answer. Of which, we said at first, that in such questions, nothing becomes a Christian better than sobriety; to make a true difference between problematical and dogmatical points, between upper buildings and foundations, between collateral doctrines and doctrines in the right line: for fundamental things, *Sine haesitatione credantur*, They must be believed without disputing. There is no more to be done for them, but believing. For things that are not so, we are to weigh them in two balances, in the balance of analogy and in the balance of scandal. We must hold them so as may be analogous, proportionate, agreeable to the articles of our faith, and we must hold them so as our brother be not justly offended nor scandalized by them. We must weigh them with faith, for our own strength, and we must weigh them with charity, for others' weakness. Certainly nothing endangers a Church more than to draw indifferent things to be necessary; I mean of a primary necessity, of a necessity to be believed *De fide*,[3] not a secondary necessity, a necessity to be performed and practised for obedience. Without doubt, the Roman Church repents now, and sees now that she should better have preserved herself if they had not denied so many particular things, which were indifferently and problematically disputed before, to be had necessarily *De fide*, in the Council of Trent.

Taking then this text for a problem, *Quis homo*, What man lives, and shall not see death? we answer, It may be that those men whom Christ shall find upon the earth alive at his return to judge the world, shall die then, and it may be they shall but be changed and not die. That Christ shall judge quick and dead is a fundamental thing; we hear it in St Peter's sermon to Cornelius and his company, and we say it every day in the Creed, He shall judge the quick and the dead. But though we do not take the quick and the dead, as Augustine and Chrysostom do, for the righteous which lived in faith, and the unrighteous which were dead in sin, though we do not take the quick and the dead, as Ruffinus and others do, for the soul and the body (He shall judge the soul, which was always alive, and He shall the body, which was dead for a time), though we take the words (as becomes us best) literally, yet the letter does not conclude, but that they whom Christ shall find alive upon earth shall have a present and sudden dissolution, and a present and sudden reunion of body and soul again. St Paul says, Behold I show you a mystery. Therefore it is not a clear case, and presently and peremptorily determined; but what is it? We shall not all sleep, but we shall all be changed. But whether this sleeping be spoke of death itself, and exclude that, that we shall not die, or whether this sleep be spoke of a rest in the grave, and exclude that, we shall not be buried and remain in death, that may be a mystery still. St Paul says too, The dead in Christ shall rise first. Then we which are alive, and remain, shall be caught up together with them in the clouds, to meet the Lord in the air. But whether that may not still be true, that St Augustine says, that there shall be *Mors in raptu*, An instant and sudden disunion, and reunion of body and soul, which is death, who can tell? So on the other side, when it is said to him, in whom all we were, to Adam, *Pulvis es*, Dust thou art, and into dust thou shalt return, when it is said, In Adam all die, when it is said, Death passed upon all men, for all have sinned, why may not all those sentences of Scripture, which imply a necessity of dying, admit that restriction, *Nisi dies judicii naturae cursum immutet*, We shall all die, except those in whom the coming of Christ shall change the course of Nature.

Consider the Scriptures then, and we shall be absolutely concluded neither way. Consider Authority, and we shall find the Fathers for the most part one way, and the School for the most part another. Take later men and all those in the Roman Church; then Cajetan thinks that they shall not die, and Catharin is so peremptory that they shall, as that he says of the other opinion, *Falsam esse confidenter asserimus, & contra Scripturas satis manifestas, & omnino sine ratione*; It is false, and against Scriptures, and reason, says he. Take later men and all those in the reformed Church; and Calvin says, *Quia aboletur prior natura, censetur species mortis, sed non migrabit anima à corpore*: St Paul calls it death, because it is a destruction of the former being; but it is not truly death, says Calvin; and Luther saith that St Paul's purpose in that place is only to show the suddenness of Christ's coming to judgement, *Non autem inficiatur omnes morituros; nam dormire, est sepeliri*. But St Paul doth not deny but that all shall die; for that sleeping which he speaks of is burial; and all shall die, though all shall not be buried, saith Luther.

Take then that which is certain: it is certain a judgement thou must pass. If thy close and cautelous proceeding have saved thee from all informations in the Exchequer, thy clearness of thy title from all courts at common law, thy moderation from the Chancery, and Star-Chamber, if height of thy place, and authority, have saved thee even from the tongues of men, so that ill men dare not slander thy actions, nor good men dare not discover thy actions, no not to thyself, all those judgements, and all the judgements of the world, are but interlocutory judgements. There is a final judgement, *In judicantes & judicatos*, against prisoners and judges too, where all shall be judged again; *Datum est omne judicium*. All judgement is given to the Son of man, and upon all the sons of men must his judgement pass. A judgement is certain, and the uncertainty of this judgement is certain too. Perchance God will put off thy judgement; thou shalt not die yet; but who knows whether God in his mercy do put off this judgement, till these good motions which his blessed Spirit inspires into thee now may take root and receive growth and bring forth fruit, or whether he put it off for a heavier judgement, to let thee see, by thy departing from these good motions and returning to thy former sins after a remorse conceived against those sins, that thou art inexcusable even to thyself, and thy condemnation is just, even to thine own conscience. So perchance God will bring this judgement upon thee now; now thou may die; but whether God will bring that judgement upon thee now, in mercy, whilst his Graces, in his ordinance of preaching, work some tenderness in thee, and give thee some preparation, some fitness, some courage to say, *Veni Domine Iesu*, Come Lord Jesu, come quickly, come now, or whether he will come now in judgement, because all this can work no tenderness in thee, who can tell?

Thou hearest the word of God preached, as thou hearest an oration, with some gladness in thyself, if thou canst hear him, and never be moved by his oratory; thou thinkest it a degree of wisdom, to be above persuasion; and when thou art told that he that fears God fears nothing else, thou thinkest thyself more valiant then so, if thou fear not God neither. Whether or why God defers or hastens the judgement we know not; This is certain, this all St Paul's places collineate to, this all the Fathers and all the School, all the Cajetans and all the Catharins, all the Luthers and all the Calvins agree in: A judgement must be, and it must be *In ictu oculi*, In the twinkling of an eye, and *Fur in nocte*, A thief in the night. Make the question, *Quis homo?* What man is he that liveth and shall not pass this judgement? Or, what man is he that liveth and knows when this judgement shall be? So it is a *Nemo scit*, A question without an answer; but ask it as in the text, *Quis homo?* Who liveth and shall not die? so it is a problematic matter; and in such things as are problematical, if thou love the peace of Sion, be not too inquisitive to know, nor too vehement, when thou thinkest thou dost know it.

Come then to ask this question, not problematically (as it is contracted to them that shall live in the last days), nor peremptorily of man (as he is subject to original sin), but at large, so as the question may include Christ himself; and then to that *Quis homo?* What man is he? we answer directly, Here is the man that shall not see death. And of him principally, and literally, St Augustine (as we said before) takes this question to be framed; *Ut quaeras, dictum, non ut desperes*, saith he: this question is moved to move thee to seek out and to have thy recourse to that man which is the Lord of Life, not to make thee despair that there is no such man, in whose self, and in whom, for all us, there is redemption from death. For, says he, this question is an exception to that which was said before the text; which is, Wherefore hast thou made all men in vain? Consider it better, says the Holy Ghost, here, and it will not prove so. Man is not made in vain at first, though he do die now; for, *Perditio tua ex te*, This death proceeds from man himself; and *Quare moriemini domus Israel?* Why will ye die, O house of Israel? God made not death, neither hath he pleasure in the destruction of the living. The Wise man says it, and the true God swears it: As I live saith the Lord, I would not the death of a sinner. God did not create man in vain then, though he die; not in vain, for since he will needs die, God receives glory even by his death, in the execution of his justice; not in vain neither, because though he be dead, God hath provided him a Redeemer from death, in his mercy; Man is not created in vain at all; nor all men so near vanity as to die; for here is one man, God and Man Christ Jesus, which lives, and shall not see death. And conformable to St Augustine's purpose speaks St Jerome too: *Scio quòd nullus homo carneus evadet, sed novi Deum sub velamento carnis latentem*; I know there is no man but shall die; but I know where there is a God clothed in man's flesh, and that person cannot die.

But did not Christ die then? Shall we join with any of those heretics which brought Christ upon the stage to play a part, and say he was born or lived or died, *In phantasmate*, In appearance only, and representation? God forbid. So all men were created in vain indeed, if we had not in him a regeneration in his true death. Where is the contract between him, and his Father, that *Oportuit pati*, All this Christ ought to suffer, and so enter into glory? Is that contract void, and of none effect? Must he not die? Where is the ratification of that contract in all the Prophets? Where is *Esays Vere languores nostros tulit*, Surely he hath born our sorrows; and he made his grave with the wicked in his death. Is the ratification of the Prophets cancelled? Shall he not, must he not die? Where is the consummation and the testification of all this? Where is the Gospel, *Consummatum est*? And he bowed his head, and gave up the ghost? Is that fabulous? Did he not die? How stands the validity of that contract, Christ must die; the dignity of those prophecies, Christ will die; the truth of the Gospel, Christ did die, with this answer to this question, Here is a man that liveth and shall not see death? Very well. For though Christ Jesus did truly die, so as was contracted, so as was prophesied, so as was related, yet he did not die so, as was intended in this question, so as other natural men do die.

For first, Christ died because he would die. Other men admitted to the dignity of martyrdom are willing to die; but they die by the torments of the executioners, they cannot bid their souls go out, and say, Now I will die. And this was Christ's case: it was not only, I lay down my life for my sheep, but he says also, No man can take away my soul and, I have power to lay it down; and *de facto*, he did lay it down, he did die, before the torments could have extorted his soul from him. Many crucified men lived many days upon the cross; the thieves were alive, long after Christ was dead; and therefore Pilate wondered that he was already dead. His soul did not leave his body by force, but because he would, and when he would, and how he would. Thus far then first, this is an answer to this question, *Quis homo?* Christ did not die naturally, nor violently, as all others do, but only voluntarily.

Again, the penalty of death appertaining only to them who were derived from Adam by carnal and sinful generation, Christ Jesus being conceived miraculously of a Virgin, by the over-shadowing of the Holy Ghost, was not subject to the law of death; and therefore in his person, it is a true answer to this *Quis homo?* Here is a man that shall not see death, that is, he need not see death, he hath not incurred God's displeasure, he is not involved in a general rebellion, and therefore is not involved in the general mortality, not included in the general penalty. He needed not have died by the rigour of any law, all we must. He could not die by the malice, or force of any execu-tioner, all we must; at least by Nature's general executioners, age and sickness. And then, when out of his own pleasure, and to advance our salvation, he would die, yet he died so as that though there were a disunion of body and soul (which is truly death), yet there remained a nobler and faster union than that of body and soul, the Hypostatical Union of the Godhead, not only to his soul, but to his body too; so that even in his death, both parts were still not only inhabited by but united to the Godhead itself; and in respect of that inseparable union, we may answer to this question, *Quis homo?* Here is a man that shall not see death, that is, he shall see no separation of that which is incomparably, and incomprehensibly, a better soul than his soul, the Godhead, shall not be separated from his body.

But that which is indeed the most direct and literal answer to this question is, that whereas the death in this text is intended of such a death as hath dominion over us, and from which we have no power to raise ourselves, we may truly and fully answer to his *Quis homo?* Here is a man that shall never see death so, but that he shall even in the jaws and teeth of death, and in the bowels and womb of the grave, and in the sink and furnace of Hell itself, retain an almighty power, and an effectual purpose, to deliver his soul from death, by a glorious, a victorious and a triumphant resurrection. So it is true, Christ Jesus died, else none of us could live; but yet he died not so as is intended in this question: not by the necessity of any law, not by the violence of any executioner, not by the separation of his best soul (if we may so call it), the Godhead, nor by such a separation of his natural and human soul, as that he would not, or could not, or did not resume it again.

If then this question had been asked of angels at first, *Quis Angelus?* What angel is that that stands and shall not fall? though as many of those angels as were disposed to that answer, *Erimus similes Altissimo*, We will be like God, and stand of ourselves, without any dependence upon him, did fall, yet otherwise they might have answered the question fairly: All we may stand, if we will. If this question had been asked of Adam in Paradise, *Quis homo?* though when he harkened to her who had harkened to that voice, *Eritis sicut Dii*, *You shall be as Gods*, he fell too, yet otherwise, he might have answered the question fairly so: I may live, and not die, if I will. So, if this question be asked of us now, as the question implies the general penalty, as it considers us only as the sons of Adam, we have no other answer, but that by Adam sin entered upon all, and death by sin upon all; as it implies the state of them only, whom Christ at his second coming shall find upon earth, we have no other answer but a modest *non liquet*, we are not sure, whether we shall die then or no. We are only sure it shall be so as most conduces to our good and God's glory; but as the question implies us to be members of our Head, Christ Jesus, as it was a true answer in him, it is true in every one of us, adopted in him: Here is a man that liveth, and shall not see death.

Death and life are in the power of the tongue, says Solomon, in another sense; and in this sense too, if my tongue, suggested by my heart, and by my heart rooted in faith, can say, *Non moriar, non moriar*,[4] if I can say (and my conscience do not tell me that I belie my own state), if I can say that the blood of my Saviour runs in my veins, that the breath of his Spirit quickens all my purposes, that all my deaths have their resurrection, all my sins their remorses, all my rebellions their reconciliations, I will harken no more after this question, as it is intended *de morte naturali*, of a natural death. I know I must die that death; what care I? Nor *de morte spirituali*, the death of sin. I know I do and shall die so; why despair I? But I will find out another death, *mortem raptus*, a death of rapture and of ecstasy, that death which St Paul died more than once. The death which St Gregory speaks of, *Divina contemplatio quoddam sepulchrum animae*, The contemplation of God, and heaven, is a kind of burial, and sepulchre, and rest of the soul; and in this death of rapture and ecstasy, in this death of the contemplation of my interest in my Saviour, I shall find myself and all my sins interred, and entombed in his wounds, and like a lily in Paradise, out of red earth, I shall see my soul rise out of his blade, in a candour and in an innocence, contracted there, acceptable in the sight of his Father.

Though I have been dead, in the delight of sin, so that that of St Paul, That a widow that liveth in pleasure, is dead while she liveth, be true of my soul, that so, *viduatur, gratiâ mortuâ*, when Christ is dead, not for the soul, but in the soul, that the soul has no sense of Christ, *Viduatur anima*, the soul is a widow, and no dowager, she has lost her husband, and hath nothing from him; yea though I have made a covenant with death, and have been at an agreement with Hell, and in a vain confidence have said to myself that when the overflowing scourge shall pass through, it shall not come to me, yet God shall annul that covenant; he shall bring that scourge, that is, some medicinal correction upon me, and so give me a participation of all the stripes of his son; he shall give me a sweat, that is, some horror and religious fear, and so give me a participation of his agony; he shall give me a diet, perchance want and penury, and so a participation of his fasting; and if he draw blood, if he kill me, all this shall be but *Mors raptus*, a death of rapture towards him, into a heavenly and assured contemplation, that I have a part in all his passion, yea such an entire interest in his whole passion, as though all that he did, or suffered, had been done and suffered for my soul alone. *Quasi moriens, & ecce vivo*; some show of death I shall have, for I shall sin; and some show of death again, for I shall have a dissolution of this tabernacle. *Sed ecce vivo*, still the Lord of life will keep me alive, and that with an *Ecce*, Behold, I live; that is, he will declare and manifest my blessed state to me. I shall not sit in the shadow of death; no nor shall I not sit in darkness; his gracious purpose shall evermore be upon me, and I shall ever discern that gracious purpose of his. I shall not die, nor I shall not doubt that I shall. If I be dead within doors (if I have sinned in my heart), why, *Suscitavit in domo*, Christ gave a resurrection to the ruler's daughter within doors, in the house. If I be dead in the gate (if I have sinned in the gates of my soul), in mine eyes or ears or Hands, in actual sins, why, *Suscitavit in porta*, Christ gave a resurrection to the young man at the gate of Naim. If I be dead in the grave (in customary and habitual sins), why, *Suscitavit in Sepulchro*, Christ gave a resurrection to Lazarus in the grave too. If God give me *mortem raptus*, a death of rapture, of ecstasy, of fervent contemplation of Christ Jesus, a transfusion, a transplantation, a transmigration, a transmutation into him (for good digestion brings always assimilation, certainly, if I come to a true meditation upon Christ, I come to a conformity with Christ), this is principally that *Pretiosa mors Sanctorum*, Precious in the sight of the Lord, is the death of his Saints, by which they are dead and buried, and risen again in Christ Jesus; precious is that death by which we apply that precious blood to ourselves, and grow strong enough by it to meet David's question, *Quis homo?* What man? with Christ's answer, *Ego homo*, I am the man, in whom whosoever abides, shall not see death.

A Lent Sermon

20th February 1629

Preached at Whitehall

> So speak ye, and so do, as they that shall be judged
> by the law of liberty.
> James 2:12

This is one of the seven epistles which Athanasius and Origen called catholic, that is, universal, perchance because they are not directed to any one Church, as some others are, but to all the Christian world. And St Jerome called them canonical, perchance because all rules, all canons of holy conversation, are comprised in these epistles. And Epiphanius and Oecumenius called them circular, perchance because as in a circle, you cannot discern which was the first point, nor in which the compass began the circle; so neither can we discern in these epistles, whom the Holy Ghost begins withal, whom he means principally, king or subject, priest or people, single or married, husband or wife, father or children, masters or servants; but universally, promiscuously, indifferently, they give all rules, for all actions, to all persons, at all times, and in all places. As in this text, in particular, which is not, by any precedent, or subsequent relation, by any connexion or coherence, directed upon any company or any degree of men: for the Apostle does not say, Ye princes, nor ye people; but ye, ye in general, to all, So speak ye, and so do, as they that shall be judged by the law of liberty. So these epistles are catholic, so they are canonical, and they are circular so. But yet, though in a circle we know not where the compass began, we know not which was the first point, yet we know that the last point of the circle returns to the first, and so becomes all one; and as much as we know the last, we know the first point. Since then the last point of that circle, in which God hath created us to move, is a kingdom (for it is the kingdom of Heaven) and it is a court (for it is that glorious court which is the presence of God, in the communion of his Saints) it is a fair and pious conception, for this congregation, here present now in this place, to believe that the first point of this circle of our Apostle here is a court too; and that the Holy Ghost, in pro-posing these duties in his general *Ye*, does principally intend ye that live in court, ye whom God brings so near to the sight of himself and of his court in Heaven, as that you have always the picture of himself and the portraiture of his court in your eyes: for a religious king is the image of God, and a religious court is a copy of the communion of Saints. And therefore be you content to think that to you especially our Apostle says here, *Ye, ye* who have a nearer propinquity to God, a more assiduous conversation with God, by having better helps than other inferior stations do afford (for though God be seen in a weed, in a worm, yet he is seen more clearly in the sun): So speak ye, and so do, as they that shall be judged by the law of liberty.

Now, as the first devils were in Heaven (for it was not the punishment which they feel in Hell, but the sin which they committed in Heaven which made them devils) and yet the fault was not in God, nor in the place; so if the greatest sins be committed in courts (as even in Rome, where they will needs have an innocent Church, yet they confess a guilty court) the faults are personal, theirs that do them, and there is no higher author of their sin. The Apostle does not bid us say that it is so in the courts; but lest it should come to be so, he bids us give these rules to courts: So speak ye, and so do, as they that shall be judged by the law of liberty. First then, here is no express precept given, no direct commandment, to speak. The Holy Ghost saw there would be speaking enough in courts; for, though there may be a great sin in silence, a great prevarication in not speaking in a good cause, or for an oppressed person, yet the lowest voice in a court, whispering itself, speaks aloud and reaches far; and therefore, here is only a rule to regulate our speech: *Sic loquimini*, So speak ye. And then, as here is no express precept for speaking, so here is no express precept for doing. The Holy Ghost saw there would be doing enough, business enough in court: for, as silence, and half silence, whispering, may have a loud voice, so, even undoing may be a busy doing; and therefore, here's only a rule to regulate our doings too: *Sic facite*, So do ye. And lastly, as there is speaking enough even in silence, and doing enough even in undoing in court, so the court is always under judgement enough. Every discontented person that hath missed his preferment, though he have not merited it; every drunkard that is over-heat, though not with his own wine; every conjecturing person that is not within the distance to know the ends, or the ways of great actions, will judge the highest counsels, and executions of those counsels. The court is under judgement enough, and they take liberty enough; and therefore here is a rule to regulate our liberty: A law of liberty: So speak ye, and, &c. But though for the more benefit of the present congregation, we fix the first point of this circle, that is, the principal purpose of the Holy Ghost, upon the court, yet our text is an amphitheatre. An amphitheatre consists of two theatres; our text hath two parts, in which all men, all may sit and see themselves acted. First, in the obligation that is laid upon us, upon us all: *Sic loquimini, sic facite*. And then in the reason of this holy diligence, and religious cautelousness: *Quia judicandi*, Because you are all to be judged, *by*, &c. Which two general parts, the obligation and the reason, flowing into many sub-divided branches, I shall, I think, do better service, both to your understandings and to your memory, and to your affections and consciences, to present them as they shall arise anon, in their order, than to pour them out, all at once now.

First then, in our first part, we look to our rule in the first duty, our speaking: *Sic loquimini*, So speak ye. The Comic Poet gives us a good caution: *Si servus semper consuescat silentio, fiet nequam*; That servant that says nothing, thinks ill. As our *Nullifidians*, Men that put all upon works, and no faith; and our *Solifidians*, Men that put all upon faith and no works, are both in the wrong; so there is a danger in *multi-loquio* and another in *nulli-loquio*: He that speaks over-freely to me, may be a man of dangerous conversation. And the silent and reserved man who makes no play but observes, and says nothing, may be more dangerous than he. As the Roman emperor professed to stand more in fear of one pale man, and lean man, than of twenty that studied and pursued their pleasures and loved their ease, because such would be glad to keep things in their state they then were, but the other sort affected changes, so for the most part he that will speak lies as open to me as I to him; speech is the balance of conversation. Therefore, as gold is not *Merx* but *pretium*; Gold is not ware but the price of all ware; so speaking is not doing, but yet fair speaking prepares an acceptation before, and puts a value after, upon the best actions. God hath made other creatures *Gregalia*, sociable, besides man: sheep and deer and pigeons will flock and herd and troop and meet together; but when they are met, they are not able to tell one another why they meet. Men only can speak; silence makes it but a herding. That that makes conversation is speech. *Qui datum deserit, respuit datorem*, says Tertullian: he that uses not a benefit reproaches his benefactor. To declare God's goodness that hath enabled us to speak, we are bound to speak, we are bound to speak: speech is the glue, the cement, the soul of conversation, and of religion too.

Now, your *conversation is in Heaven*; and therefore *loquimini Deo*, first speak to him that is in Heaven, speak to God. Some of the Platonic philosophers thought it a profanation of God to speak to God. They thought that when our thoughts were made prayers, and that the heart flowed into the tongue, and that we had invested and apparelled our meditations with words, this was a kind of painting and dressing and a superfluous diligence that rather tasted of humane affections than such a sincere service as was fit for the presence of God. Only the first conceptions, the first ebullitions and emanations of the soul, in the heart, they thought to be a fit sacrifice to God, and all verbal prayer to be too homely for him. But God himself, who is all spirit, hath yet put on bodily lineaments, head and hands and feet, yea and garments too, in many places of Scripture, to appear, that is, to manifest himself to us. And when we appear to God, though our Devotion be all spiritual, as he is all spirit, yet let us put on lineaments and apparel upon our devotions, and digest the meditations of the heart into words of the mouth. God came to us *in verbo*, In the word; for Christ is the word that was made flesh. Let us that are Christians go to God so, too, that the words of our mouth, as well as the meditations of our heart, may be acceptable to him. Surely, God loves the service of prayer, or he would never have built a house for prayer. And therefore we justly call public prayer, the liturgy, service: love that place, and love that service in that place, prayer. They will needs make us believe that St Francis preached to birds and beasts and stones, but they will not go about to make us believe that those birds and beasts and stones joined with St Francis in prayer. God can speak to all things; that's the office of preaching, to speak to others. But, of all, only man can speak to God; and that's the office of prayer. It is a blessed conversation, to spend time in discourse, in communication with God. God went his way, as soon as he had left communing with Abraham. When we leave praying, God leaves us. But God left not Abraham, as long as he had anything to say to God. And we have always something to say unto him. He loves to hear us tell him even those things which he knew before: his benefits in our thankfulness, and our sins in our confessions, and our necessities in our petitions. And therefore having so many occasions to speak to God, and to speak of God, David ingeminates that, and his ingemination implies a wonder: O that men would (And it is strange if men will not) O that men would, says he more than once or twice, O that men would praise the Lord, and tell the wondrous works that he hath done for the sons of men! For David determines not his precept in that, Be thankful unto him; for a thankfulness may pass in private, but Be thankful unto him, and speak good of his name. Glorify him in speaking to him, in speaking of him, in speaking for him.

Loquimini Deo, speak to God. And *loquimini Diis*, speak to them whom God hath called gods. As religious kings are bound to speak to God by way of prayer, so those who have that sacred office, and those that have that honourable office to do so, are bound to speak to kings by way of counsel. God hath made all good men partakers of the Divine Nature; they are the sons of God, the seed of God. But God hath made kings partakers of his office and administration. And as between man and himself God hath put a mediator that consists of God and man, so between princes and people God hath put mediators too, who considered in themselves retain the nature of the people (so Christ did of man) but considered in their places have fair and venerable beams of his power, and influences of him upon them. And as our mediator Christ Jesus found always his Father's ears open to him, so do the Church and State enter blessedly and success- fully, by these mediators, into the ears of the king. Of our mediator Christ himself, it is said, That he offered up prayers, and strong cries, and tears. Even Christ was put to some dif- ficulties in his mediation for those that were his. But he was heard, says that text, in that he feared. Even in those things wherein, in some emergent difficulties, they may be afraid they shall not, these mediators are graciously and opportunely heard too, in the due discharge of their offices. That which was David's prayer is our possession, our happiness: Let not the foot of pride come against us. We know there is no pride in the head; and because there is no fault in the hands neither, that is, in them, into whose hands this blessed mediatorship is committed, by the great places of power, and counsel, which they worthily hold, the foot of pride, foreign or home-oppression does not, shall not tread us down. And for the continuation of happiness, let me have leave to say, with Mordicai's humility, and earnestness too, to all such mediators, that which he said to Esther: Who knows, whether thou beest not brought to this place for this purpose? To speak that which his sacred and gracious ears, to whom thou speakest, will always be well pleased to hear, when it is delivered by them to whom it belongs to speak it, and in such humble and reserved manner, as such sovereign persons as owe an account but to God, should be spoke too? *Sic loquimini Deo*, So let kings speak to God (that was our first), *Sic loquimini Diis*, So let them, whom kings trust, speak to kings, whom God hath called gods (that was our second). And then a third branch in this rule of our first duty is, *Sic loquimini imaginibus Dei*, So speak you to God's images, to men of condition inferior to yourselves; for they also are images of God, as you are.

And this is truly, most literally the purpose of the Apostle here, that you under-value no man for his outward appearance, that you over-value no man for his goodly apparel or gold rings; that you say not to a poor man, Stand thou there; or as you admit him to sit, Sit here under my footstool. But it is a precept of accessibleness and of affability: affability, that is, a civility of the City of God, and a courtship of the court of Heaven, to receive other men, the images of God, with the same easiness that God receives you. God stands at the door and knocks and stays at our leisure, to see if we will open and let him in. Even at the door of his Beloved, he stood, and knocked, till his head was filled with dew, and his locks with the drops of the night. But God puts none of us to that to which he puts himself and his Christ. But, Knock, says he, and it shall be opened unto you; no staying at the door, opened as soon as you knock. The nearest that our expositors can come to find what it was that offended God, in Moses' striking of the rock for water, is that he struck it twice, that he did not believe that God would answer his expectation at one striking. God is no inaccessible god, that he may not be come to; nor inexorable, that he will not be moved, if he be spoken to; nor dilatory, that he does not that he does seasonably.

Daniel presents God *Antiquum Dierum*, as an old man, but that is as a reverend, not as a froward person. *Mens in sermonibus nostris habitat, & gubernat verba*: The soul of man is incorporate in his words. As he speaks, we think he thinks: *Et bonus paterfamilias, in illo primo vestibulo æstimatur*, says the same Father. As we believe that to be a free house where there is an easy entrance, so we doubt the less of a good heart, if we find charitable and courteous language. But yet there is an excess in this too, in this self-effusion, this pouring of a man's self out, in fair and promising language. Inaccessibleness is the fault which the Apostle aims at here, and truly the most inaccessible man that is is the over-liberal and profuse promiser. He is therefore the most inaccessible, because he is absent when I am come to him and when I do speak with him. To a retired, to a reserved man, we do not easily get; but when we are there, he is there too. To an open and liberal promiser we get easily; but when we are with him, he is away, because his heart, his purpose is not there. But, *sic loquimini Deo*, so speak ye to God (that's a remembrance to kings); *Sic loquimini Diis*, so speak ye to them whom God hath called gods (that's a remembrance to mediators between kings and subjects); *Sic loquimini Imaginibus Dei*, so speak ye to God's images, to all men (that's a remembrance to all that possess any superiority over others) as that your *loquimini* may be accompanied with a *facite*, your saying with doing, your good words with good actions. For so our Apostle joins them here, *So speak ye, and so do*. And so we are come to our second rule: from the rule of our words to the rule of our actions.

John the Baptist was all voice, yet John the Baptist was a fore-runner of Christ. The best words are but words, but they are the fore-runners of deeds. But Christ himself, as he was God himself, is *Purus actus*, all action, all doing. Comfortable words are good cordials; they revive the spirits and they have the nature of such occasional physic; but deeds are our food, our diet, and that that constantly nourishes us. *Non verbo*, says the

Apostle: let us not love in word nor in tongue, but in deed and in truth. Not that we may not love in words, but that our deeds are the true seals of that love, which was also love when it was in words. But *Ne quod luxuriat in flore, attenuetur & hebetetur in fructu*; lest that tree that blew early and plentifully blast before it knit, second your good words with actions too. It is the husbandry and the harvest of the righteous man; (as it is gathered in David) The mouth of the righteous speaketh wisdom: so we read it; there it is in the tongue, in words only. The vulgar hath it *Meditatur*, He meditates it; so the heart is got in. But the original, *Hagah*, is noted to signify *fructificavit*, He brings forth fruits thereof; and so the hand is got in too. And when that which is well spoken was well meant and hath been well expressed in action, that's the husbandry of the righteous man; then his harvest is all in. It is the way of God himself: Philo Judæus notes that the people are said to have seen the noise and the voice of God; because, whatever God says, it determines in action. If we may hear God, we may see him; what he says, he does too. Therefore from that example of God himself, St Gregory directs us: we must, says he, show our love, *Et veneratione sermonis, & Ministerio largitatis*, with a fair respect in words, and with a real supply in deeds. Nay, when we look upon our pattern, that is, God, Tertullian notes well that God prevented his own speaking by doing; *Benedicebat, quæ benefaciebat*; first he made all things good and then he blessed them that they might be better; first he wrought and then he spoke. And so Christ's ways and proceeding is presented to us too: so far from not doing when he speaks as that he does before he speaks. Christ began to do and to teach, says St Luke; but first to do. And He was mighty in deeds and in words, but first in deeds. We cannot write so well as our copy, to begin always at deeds, as God and His Christ. But yet let us labour to write so fair after it, as first to afford comfortable words; and though our Deeds come after, yet to have them from the beginning in our intention; and that we do them, not because we promised, but promise because we love to do good, and love to lay upon ourselves the obligation of a promise. The instrument and organ of Nature was the eye; the natural man finds God in that he sees, in the creature. The organ of the law, which exalted and rectified Nature, was the hand: *Fac hoc & vives*; perform the law and thou shalt live. So also, the organ of the Gospel is the ear, for faith comes by hearing. But then the organ of faith itself is the hand too: a hand that lays hold upon the merits of Christ for myself, and a hand that delivers me over to the Church of God, in a holy life and exemplary actions for the edification of others. So that all, all from Nature to grace determines in action, in doing good. *Sic facite Deo*, so do good to God, in real assisting his cause; *Sic facite Diis*, so do good to them whom God hath called gods, in real seconding their religious purposes. *Sic facite Imaginibus Dei*, so do good to the images of God, in real relieving his distressed members, as that you do all this, upon that which is made the reason of all, in the second part of this text. Because you are to be judged by the law of liberty.

Timor futuri judicii hujus vitæ pædagogus, Our schoolmaster to teach us to stand upright in the last judgement, is the meditation, and the fear of that judgement, in this life. It is our schoolmaster and schoolmaster enough. I said unto this fool thus and thus, says David, And I said unto the wicked thus and thus, says he: for, says he, God is the judge. He thought it enough to enlighten the understanding of the fool, enough to rectify the perverseness of the wicked, if he could set God before them in that notion, as a judge. For this is one great benefit from the present contemplation of the future judgement, that whosoever does truly and advisedly believe that ever he shall come to judgement is at it now; he that believes that God will judge him is God's commissioner, God's delegate, and, in his name, judges himself now. Therefore it is a useful mistaking which the Roman translation is fallen into, in this text, in reading it thus: *Sicut incipientes judicari*; So speak ye, and so do, as they upon whom the judgement were already begun. For,

Qui timet ante Christi Tribunal præsentari, He that is afraid to be brought to the last judgement, hath but one refuge, but one sanctuary: *Ascendat Tribunal Mentis suæ & constitutat se ante seipsum*; Let him cite himself before himself, give evidence himself against himself; and so guilty as he is found here, so innocent he shall stand there. Let him proceed upon himself, as Job did, and he is safe: I am afraid of all my sorrow*s*, says he; afraid that I have not said enough against myself nor repented enough, afraid that my sorrows have not been sincere, but mingled with circumstances of loss of health or honour or fortune occasioned by my sins; and not only, not principally, for the sin itself. I am afraid of all my sorrows, says he, but how much more then of my mirths and pleasures? To judge ourselves by the judgement of flatterers that depend upon us, to judge ourselves by the event and success of things (I am enriched, I am preferred by this course and therefore all's well), to judge ourselves by example of others (others do thus, and why not I?), all these proceedings are *Coram non Judice*, all these are literally *Præmunire* cases, for they are appellations into foreign jurisdictions and foreign judicatures. Only our own conscience rectified is a competent judge. And they that have passed the trial of that judgement do not so much rise to judgement at last as stand and continue in judgement. Their judgement, that is, their trial, is passed here; and there they shall only receive sentence, and that sentence shall be, *Euge bone serve*; Well done good and faithful servant; since thou didst enter into our judgement in the other world, enter into thy Master's joy in this. But howsoever we be prepared for that judgement, well or not well, and howsoever the judge be disposed towards us, well or not well, there is this comfort given us here, that that judgement shall be *per legem*, by a law; we shall be judged by a law of liberty, which is our second branch in this second part.

The Jews that prosecuted the judgement against Christ durst not do that without pretending a law: *Habemus legem*, say they, we have a law, and he hath transgressed that. The necessary precipitations into sudden executions to which states are forced in rebellious times we are fain to call by the name of law, martial law. The torrents and inundations which invasive armies pour upon nations we are fain to call by the name of law, the law of arms. No judgement, no execution, without the name, the colour, the pretence of law; for still men call for a law for every execution. And shall not the judge of all the earth do right? Shall God judge us, condemn us, execute us, execute us at the last day, and not by a law? By something that we never saw, never knew, never notified, never published, and judge me by that, and leave out the consideration of that law which he bound me to keep? I ask St Paul's question: Where is the disputer of the world? Who will offer to dispute unnecessary things, especially where authority hath made it necessary to us to forbear such disputations? Blessed are the peace-makers that command and blessed are the peace-keepers that obey and accommodate themselves to peace, in forbearing unnecessary and uncharitable controversies. But without controversy, great is the mystery of godliness. The Apostle invites us to search into no further mysteries than such as may be without controversy; the mystery of godliness is without controversy, and godliness is to believe that God hath given us a law, and to live according to that law. This, this godliness (that is, knowledge and obedience to the law) hath the promises of this life, and the next too, all referred to his law. For, without this, this godliness (which is holiness) no man shall see God: all referred to a law. This is Christ's catechism in St John, that we might know the only true God, and Jesus Christ whom he sent. A God commanding, and a Christ reconciling us, if we have transgressed that commandment. And this is the Holy Ghost's catechism in St Paul: *Deus remunerator*, That we believe God to be, and to be a just rewarder of man's actions: still all referred to an obedience or disobedience of a law. The mystery of godliness is great, that is, great enough for our salvation, and yet without controversy; for though controversies have been moved about God's first act, there can be none of his last act;

though men have disputed of the object of election, yet of this subject of execution there is no controversy. No man can doubt but that when God delivers over any soul actually, and by way of execution, to eternal condemnation, that he delivers over that soul to that eternal condemnation for breaking his law. In this we have no other adversary but the over-sad, the despairing soul; and it becomes us all to lend our hand to his succour, and to pour in our wine and our oil into his wounds, that lies weltering and surrounded in the blood of his own pale and exhausted soul. That soul who though it can testify to itself some endeavour in the ways of holiness, yet upon some collateral doubts is still suspicious, and jealous of God. How often have we seen that a needless jealousy and suspicion, conceived without a cause, hath made a good body bad? A needless jealousy and suspicion of his purposes and intentions upon thee may make thy merciful God angry too. Nothing can alienate God more from thee than to think that anything but sin can alienate him. How wouldst thou have God merciful to thee if thou wilt be unmerciful to God himself? And, *Qui quid tyrannicum in Deo*, He that conceives any tyrannical act in God, is unjust to the God of Justice, and unmerciful to the God of Mercy. Therefore in the 17th of our injunctions, we are commanded to arm sad souls against despair by setting forth the mercy and the benefits and the godliness of Almighty God (as the word of the injunction is, the godliness of God) for to leave God under a suspicion of dealing ill with any penitent soul were to impute ungodliness to God. Therefore to that mistaking soul, that discomposed, that shivered and shrivelled and ravelled and ruined soul, to that jealous and suspicious soul only, I say with the Apostle, *Let no man judge you*, intruding into those things which he hath not seen. Let no man make you afraid of secret purposes in God which they have not nor you have not seen; for that by which you shall be judged is the law, that law which was notified and published to you. The law alone were much too heavy if there were not a superabundant ease and alleviation in that hand that Christ Jesus reaches out to us. O consider the weight and the ease; and for pity to such distrustful souls, and for establishment of your own, stop your devotions a little upon this consideration. First, there is *Chirographum*, a handwriting of ordinances against me; a debt, an obligation contracted by our first parents, in their disobedience, and fallen upon me. And even that (be it but original sin) is shrewd evidence; there's my first charge. But, *Deletum est*, says the Apostle there: that's blotted, that's defaced, that cannot be sued against me, after baptism. Nay, *Sublatum, cruci affixum*, it is cancelled, it is nailed to the Cross of Christ Jesus, it is no more sin; in itself it is but to me, to condemnation, it is not; here's my charge, and my discharge for that. But yet there is heavier evidence, *Pactum cum inferno*, as the Prophet Esay speaks: I have made a covenant with death, and with Hell I am at an agreement; that is, says St Gregory, *Audacter, Indefinenter peccamus, & diligendo, amicitiam profitemur*: We sin constantly and we sin continually and we sin confidently; and we find so much pleasure and profit in sin as that we have made a league and sworn a friendship with sin, and we keep that perverse and irreligious promise over-religiously; and the sins of our youth flow into other sins, when age disables us for them. But yet there is *Deletum est* in this case too; our covenant with death is disannulled (says that prophet) when we are made partakers of the death of Christ, in the blessed sacrament. Mine actual sins lose their act, and mine habitual sins fall from me as a habit, as a garment put off, when I come to that: there's my charge, and my discharge for that. But yet there is worse evidence against me, than either this *Chirographum*, the first handwriting of Adam's hand, or than this *pactum*, this contract of mine own hand, actual and habitual sin (for of these, one is washed out in water, and the other in blood, in the two sacraments). But then there is *Lex in Membris*, says the Apostle, I find a law, that when I would do good, evil is present with me. Sin assisted by me is now become a tyrant over me and hath established a government upon me; and there is a law of sin and

34

a law in my flesh, which after the water of Baptism taken and the water of penitent tears given, after the blood of Jesus Christ taken and mine own blood given (that is, a holy readiness at that time, when I am made partaker of Christ's death, to die for Christ), throws me back by relapses into those repented sins. This put the Apostle to that passionate exclamation: O wretched man that I am! And yet he found a deliverance, even from the body of this death, through Jesus Christ his Lord: that is, a free, an open recourse and access to him in all oppressions of heart, in all dejections of spirit. Now, when this *Chirographum*, this bond of Adam's hand, original sin, is cancelled upon the Cross of Christ; and this *Pactum*, this bond of mine own hand, actual sins, washed away in the blood of Christ; and this *Lex in membris*, this disposition to relapse in repented sins (which, as a tide that does certainly come very day, does come every day in one form or the other) is beaten back, as a tide by a bank, by a continual opposing of the merits and the example of Christ Jesus, and the practise of his fasting, and such other medicinal disciplines as I find to prevail against such relapses; when by this blessed means, the whole law against which I am trespasser is evacuated, will God condemn me for all this, and not by a law? When I have pleaded Christ and Christ and Christ baptism and blood and tears, will God condemn me an oblique way, when he cannot by a direct way; by a secret purpose, when he hath no law to condemn me by? Sad and disconsolate, distorted and distracted soul! If it be well said in the school, *Absurdum est disputare, ex manuscriptis*, it is an unjust thing in controversies and disputations to press arguments out of manuscripts that cannot be seen by every man, it were ill said in thy conscience that God will proceed against thee *ex manuscriptis*, or condemn thee upon anything which thou never sawest, any unrevealed purpose of his. Suspicious soul! ill-presaging soul! Is there something else, besides the Day of Judgement, that the son of man does not know? Disquiet soul! Does he not know the proceeding of that judgement wherein himself is to be the judge? But that when he hath died for thy sins, and so fulfilled the law in thy behalf, thou mayest be condemned without respect of that law, and upon something that shall have had no consideration, no relation to any such breach of any such law in thee? Intricated, intangled conscience! Christ tells thee of a judgement because thou didst not do the works of mercy, not feed, not clothe the poor, for those were enjoined thee by a law. But he never tells thee of any judgement therefore because thy name was written in a dark book of death, never unclasped, never opened unto thee in thy life. He says unto thee lovingly and indulgently, Fear not, for it is God's good pleasure to give you the kingdom. But he never says to the wickedest in the world: Live in fear, die in anxiety and suspicion and suspension for his displeasure: a displeasure conceived against you, before you were sinners, before you were men, hath thrown you out of that kingdom into utter darkness. There is no condemnation to them that are in Jesus Christ; the reason is added, because the law of the spirit of life hath made them free from the law of sin and of death. All, upon all sides, is still referred to law. And where there is no law against thee (as there is not to him that is in Christ; and he is in Christ who hath endeavoured the keeping or repented the breaking of the law) God will never proceed to execution by any secret purpose never notified, never manifested. Suspicious, jealous, scattered soul, recollect thyself, and give thyself that redintegration, that acquiescence which the Spirit of God in the means of the Church offers thee. Study the mystery of godliness, which is without all controversy; that is, endeavour to keep, repent the not keeping of the law, and thou art safe; for that that you shall be judged by is a law. But then this law is called here a law of liberty; and whether that denotation, that it is called a law of liberty, import an ease to us, or a heavier weight upon us, is our last disquisition, and conclusion of all: So speak ye, and so do, as they that shall be judged by the law of liberty.

That the Apostle here by the law of liberty means the Gospel was never doubted. He had called the Gospel so, before this

place: Whoso looketh into the perfect law of liberty, and con-
tinueth therein, shall be blessed in his deed; that is, blessed in
doing so, blessed in conforming himself to the Gospel. But why
does he call it so, a law of liberty? Not because men, naturally
affecting liberty, might be drawn to an affection of the Gospel
by proposing it in that specious name of liberty, though it were
not so. The Holy Ghost calls the Gospel a pearl and a treasure
and a kingdom and joy and glory; not to allure men with false
names, but because men love these, and the Gospel is truly all
these: a pearl and a treasure and a kingdom and joy and glory.
And it is truly a law of liberty. But of what kind, and in what
respect? Not such a liberty as they have established in the
Roman Church, where ecclesiastical liberty must exempt ecclesiastical persons from participating all burdens of the State
and from being traitors, though they commit treason, because
they are subjects to no secular prince. Nor the liberty of the
Anabaptists, that overthrows magistracy and consequently all
subjection, both ecclesiastical and lay. For when upon those
words, Be ye not servants of men, St Chrysostom says, this is
Christian liberty, *Nec aliis nec sibi servire*, neither to be subject
to others, nor to ourselves; that's spoken with modification
with relation to ourselves; that's spoken with modification with
relation to our first allegiance, our allegiance to God; not to be
so subject to others, or to ourselves, as that either for their sakes
or our own, we depart from any necessary declaration of our
service to God.

First then, the Gospel is a law of liberty in respect of the
author of the Gospel, of God himself, because it leaves God at
his liberty. Not at liberty to judge against his Gospel where he
hath manifested it for a law; for he hath laid a holy necessity
upon himself to judge according to that law, where he hath
published that law. But at liberty so, as that it consists only in his
good pleasure to what nation he will publish the Gospel, or in
what nation he will continue the Gospel, or upon what persons
he will make this Gospel effectual. So Oecumenius (who is no

single witness, nor speaks not alone, but compiles the former Fathers) places this liberty in God, that God is at liberty to give this Gospel when he will; and at liberty so, as that he hath exempted no man, how well soever he love him; nor put any such fetters or manacles upon himself, but that he can and will punish those that transgress this law. So it is a law of liberty to God; nothing determined upon any man, nothing concluded in himself, lies so in God's way as to hinder him from proceeding in his last judgement, according to the keeping or breaking of this law; still God is at his liberty. And it is a law of liberty in respect of us, of us who are Christians; and considered so, either with a respect to the natural man or with a respect to the Jew. For if we compare the Christian with the natural man, the law of Nature lays the same obligation upon the natural man as the Gospel does upon the Christian, for the moral part thereof. The Christian is no more bound to love God nor his neighbour than the natural man is; therein the natural man hath no more liberty than the Christian; so far their law is equal. And then all the law which the Christian hath and the natural man hath not is a law of liberty to the Christian, that is, a law that gives him an ease, and a readier way to perform those duties; which way the natural man hath not, and yet is bound to the same duties. The natural man, if he transgress that law which he finds in his own heart, finds a condemnation in himself, as well as the Christian; therein he is no freer than the Christian. But he finds no sanctuary, no altar, no sacrifice, no church, no such liberties as the Christian does in the Gospel. So the Gospel is a law of liberty to us in respect of the natural man, that it sets us at liberty, restores us to liberty, after we are fallen into prison for debt, into God's displeasure for sin, by affording us means of reconciliation to God again.

It is so also in respect of the law given by God to the Jews. The Jews had liberties, that is, refuge and help of sacrifices for sin, which the natural man had not; for if the natural man were driven and followed from his own heart, that he saw no comfort of an innocence there, he had no other liberties to fly to, no comfort in any other thing: no law, no promise annexed to any other action; not to sacrifice, as the Jews; or to sacrament, as the Christians, but must irremediably sink under the condemnation of his own heart. The Jew had this liberty, a law, and a law that involved the Gospel; but then the Gospel was to the Jew but as a letter sealed; and the Jew was but as a servant who was trusted to carry the letter as it was, sealed, to another, to carry it to the Christian. Now the Christian hath received this letter at the Jew's hand, and he opens it; he sees the Jew's prophecy made history to him; the Jew's hope and reversion made possession and inheritance to him; he sees the Jew's faith made matter of fact. He sees all that was promised and represented in the law performed and recorded in the Gospel and applied in the Church. There Christ says, Henceforth call I you not servants, but friends. Wherein consists this enfranchisement? In this: The servant knoweth not what his master doth (the Jews knew not that) but I have called you friends, says the Apostle. Christ, for all things that I heard of my Father I have made known unto you. The law made nothing perfect, says the Apostle. Where was the defect? He tells us that: The old covenant (that is, the law) gendereth to bondage. What bondage? He tells us that too, when he says, The law was a schoolmaster. The Jews were as schoolboys, always spelling, and putting together types and figures, which things typified and figured how this lamb should signify Christ, how this fire should signify a Holy Ghost. The Christian is come from school to the university, from grammar to logic, to him that is *Logos* itself, the Word; to apprehend and apply Christ himself; and so is at more liberty than when he had only a dark law, without any comment, with the natural man; or only a dark comment, that is, the law, with a dim light and ill eyes, as the Jews had: for though the Jew had the liberty of a law, yet they had not the law of liberty. So the Gospel is a law of liberty to God, who is still at his liberty to give and take, and to condemn according to that law; and a law of liberty to us, as we are compared to the natural man, or to the Jew. But when we confine ourselves in ourselves, positively, without comparison, it is not such a law of liberty to us as some men have come too near saying: that the sins of God's children do them no harm; that God sees not the sins of his children; that God was no further out with David in his adultery than in his repentance. But as to be born within the covenant, that is, of Christian parents, does not make us Christians (for, *Non nascitur, sed renascitur Christianus*), the covenant gives us a title to the sacrament of baptism, and that sacrament makes us Christians: so this law of liberty gives us not a liberty to sin, but a liberty from sin. *Noli libertate abuti, ad libere peccandum*, says the same Father: it is not a liberty, but an impotency, a slavery, to sin. *Voluntas libera quæ pia*, says he: only a holy soul is a free soul. Where the spirit of the Lord is, there is liberty, says the Apostle. And *Splendidissimum in se quisque habet speculum*, Every man hath a glass, a crystal, into which, though he cannot call up this spirit (for the spirit of God breathes where it pleases him) yet he can see this spirit, if he be there, in that glass; every man hath a glass in himself, where he may see himself and the image of God, says that Father, and see how like he is to that. To dare to reflect upon myself, and to search all the corners of mine own conscience, whether I have rightly used this law of liberty; and neither been bold before a sin upon presumption of an easy, nor diffident after upon suspicion of an impossible reconciliation to my God. This is evangelical liberty.

So, then (to end all), though it be a law of liberty, because it gives us better means of prevention before and of restitution after than the natural man or the Jew had, yet we consider that it is this law of liberty, this law that hath afforded us these good helps, by which we shall be judged; and so, though our case be better than theirs, because we have this law of liberty which they wanted, yet our case grows heavier than theirs, if we use it not aright. The Jews shall be under a heavier condemnation than the natural man because they had more liberty, that is, more means of avoiding sin, than the natural man had; and, upon the same reason, the Christian under a heavier condemnation than either, because he shall be judged by this law of liberty.

What judgement then gives this law? This: *Qui non crediderit, damnabitur*; and so says this law in the Lawmaker's mouth: *He* that believes not shall be damned. And as no less light than faith itself can show you what faith is, what it is to believe, so no less time than damnation shall last can show you what damnation is. For, the very form of damnation is the everlastingness of it; and, *Qui non crediderit*, He that believeth not shall be damned: there's no commutation of penance, nor beheading after a sentence of a more ignominious death, in that court. Dost thou believe that thou dost believe? Yet this law takes not that answer. This law of liberty takes the liberty to look farther: Through faith into works; for, so says the law in the mouth of the Lawmaker, To whom much is given, of him much shall be required. Hast thou considered every new title of honour and every new addition of office, every new step into higher places, to have laid new duties, and new obligations upon thee? Hast thou doubled the hours of thy prayers when thy preferments are doubled, and increased thine alms according as thy revenues are increased? Hast thou done something, done much in this kind? This law will not be answered so; this law of liberty takes the liberty to call upon thee for all. Here also the law says in the mouth of the Lawmaker, If thou have agreed with many adversaries, says Christ (let that be, If thou have satisfied many duties, for duties are adversaries, that is, temptations upon us), yet, as long as thou hast one adversary, agree with that adversary quickly in the way; leave no duty undischarged or unrepented in this life. Beloved, we have well delivered ourselves of the fear of Purgatory; none of us fear that. But another mistaking hath overtaken us and we flatter ourselves with another danger, that is, compensation, that by doing well in one place, our ill doing in another is recompensed: an ill officer looks to be saved because he is a good husband to his wife, a good father to his children, a good master to his servants; and he thinks he hath three to one for his salvation. But as Nature requires the qualities of every element which thou art composed of, so this law of liberty calls upon thee for the exercises of all those virtues that appertain to every particular place thou holdest. This liberty, this law of liberty takes. It binds thee to believe Christ, all Christ, God's Christ, as he was the eternal Son of the Father, God of God; our Christ, as he was made man for our salvation; and thy Christ, as his blessed Spirit, in this his ordinance, applies him to thee, and offers him into thine arms this minute. And then, to know that he looks for a retribution from thee, in that measure in which he hath dealt with thee: much for much, and for several kinds of good, according to those several good things which he hath done for thee. And, if thou be first defective in these and then defective in laying hold upon him who is the propitiation and satisfaction for thy defects in these, this law of liberty returns to her liberty to pronounce, and the judge to his liberty to execute that sentence, *Damnaberis*, thou wilt be cast into that prison where thou must pay the last farthing. Thou must, for, Christ dies not there, and therefore there thou must lie, till there come such another ransom as Christ; nay, a greater ransom than Christ was, for Christ paid no debts in that prison. This then is the Christian's case, and this is the abridgement of his religion; *Sic loquimini, sic facite*; to speak aright and to do aright; to profess the truth, and not be afraid nor ashamed of that and to live according to that profession. For no man can make God the author of sin, but that man comes as near it as he can that makes God's religion a cloak for his sin. To this God proceeds not merely and only by commandment but by persuasion too. And, though he be not bound to do so, yet he does give a reason. The reason is, because we must give account of both: both of actions and of words; of both we shall be judged, but judged by a law, a law which excludes on God's part any secret ill purpose upon us, if we keep his law; a law which ex- cludes on our part all pretence of ignorance; for no man can plead ignorance of a law. And then a law of liberty, of liberty to

God: for God was not bound to save a man because he made him; but of his own goodness he vouchsafed him a law by which he may be saved. A law of liberty to us: so that there is no Epicurism, to do what we list, no such liberty as makes us libertines, for then there were no law; nor Stoicism, nor fatality, that constrains us to do that we would not do, for then there were no liberty. But the Gospel is such a law of liberty as delivers us, upon whom it works, from the necessity of falling into the bondage of sin before, and from the impossibility of recovering after, if we be fallen into that bondage. And this is liberty enough; and of this liberty, our blessed God give us the right use, for his Son Christ Jesus' sake, by the operation of that Holy Ghost, that proceeds from both.

Amen.

A Lent Sermon

12th February 1630

Preached to the King at Whitehall

> For, where your treasure is, there will your heart be also.
> Matthew 6:21

I have seen minute-glasses; glasses so short-lived. If I were to preach upon this text, to such a glass, it were enough for half the sermon, enough to show the worldly man his treasure and the object of his heart (for, where your treasure is, there will your heart be also), to call his eye to that minute-glass, and to tell him, there flows, there flies your treasure, and your heart with it. But if I had a secular glass, a glass that would run an age; if the two hemispheres of the world were composed in the form of such a glass, and all the world calcined and burnt to ashes, and all the ashes and sands and atoms of the world put into that glass, it would not be enough to tell the godly man what is his treasure, and the object of his heart is. A parrot or a stare,[5] docile birds and of pregnant imitation, will sooner be brought to relate to us the wisdom of a council table, than any Ambrose or any Chrysostom, men that have gold and honey in their names, shall tell us what the sweetness, what the treasure of Heaven is, and what that man's peace, that has set his heart upon that treasure. As Nature hath given us certain elements and all bodies are composed of them, and art hath given us a certain alphabet of letters and all words are composed of them, so, our blessed Saviour, in these three chapters of this Gospel, hath given us a sermon of texts of which all our sermons may be composed. All the articles of our religion, all the canons of our Church, all the injunctions of our princes, all the homilies of our fathers, all the body of divinity is in these three chapters, in this one

45

Sermon on the Mount, where, as the preacher concludes his sermon with exhortations to practice (*whosoever hears these sayings of mine, and doth them*), so he fortifies his sermon with his own practice (which is a blessed and a powerful method) for, as soon as he came out of the pulpit, as soon as he came down from the mount, he cured the first leper he saw, and that without all vainglory, for he forbade him to tell any man of it.

Of this noble body of divinity, one fair limb is in this text: Where your treasure is, there will your heart be also. Immediately before, our blessed Saviour had forbidden us the laying up of Treasure in this world upon this reason, that here moths and rust corrupt, and thieves break in and steal. There the reason is because the money may be lost; but here, in our text it is because the man may be lost: for where your treasure is, there your heart will be also. So that this is equivalent to that: What profit to gain the whole world, and lose a man's own soul? Our text therefore stands as that proverbial, that hieroglyphic letter, Pythagoras his Y, that hath first a stalk, a stem to fix itself, and then spreads into two beams. The stem, the stalk of this letter, this Y, is in the first word of the text, that particle of argumentation, For: take heed where you place your treasure, for it concerns you much, where your heart be placed; and, where your treasure is, there will your heart be also. And then opens this symbolic, this catechistical letter, this Y, into two horns, two beams, two branches: one broader, but on the left hand, denoting the treasures of this world; the other narrower, but on the right hand, treasure laid up for the world to come. Be sure you turn the right way: for, where your treasure is, there will your heart be also.

First then, we bind ourselves to the stake, to the stalk, to the staff, the stem of this symbolic letter, and consider it in that firmness and fixation of the heart which God requires. God requires no unnatural thing at man's hand; whatsoever God requires of man, man may find imprinted in his own nature, written in his own heart. This firmness then, this fixation of the heart, is natural to man. Every man does set his heart upon something, and Christ in this place does not so much call upon him that he would do so, set his heart upon something, as to be sure that he set it upon the right object. And yet truly, even this first work, to recollect ourselves, to recapitulate ourselves, to assemble and muster ourselves, and to bend our hearts entirely and intensely, directly, earnestly, emphatically, energetically, upon something is, by reason of the various fluctuation of our corrupt nature, and the infinite multiplicity of objects, such a work as man needs to be called upon and excited to do it. Therefore is there no word in the Scriptures so often added to the heart as that of entireness: *Toto Corde, Omni Corde, Pleno Corde*: Do this with all thine heart, with a whole heart, with a full heart; for whatsoever is indivisible is immoveable; a point, because it cannot be divided, cannot be moved: the centre, the poles, God himself, because he is indivisible, is therefore immoveable. And when the heart of man is knit up in such an entireness upon one object as that it does not scatter, nor subdivide itself, then, and then only, is it fixed. And that's the happiness in which David fixes himself; not in his *Cor paratum*, My heart is prepared, O God, my heart is prepared (for so it may be, prepared even by God himself, and yet scattered and subdivided by us), but in his *Cor fixum*, My heart is fixed, O God, my heart is fixed; Awake my glory, awake my psaltery and harp: I myself will awake early, and praise thee, O Lord, among the people. A triumph that David returned to more than once, for he repeats the same words with the same pathetical earnestness again. So that his glory, his victory, his triumph, his peace, his acquiescence, his all-sufficiency in himself, consisted in this, that his heart was fixed: for this fixation of the heart argued and testified an entireness in it. When God says, *Fili, da mihi Cor*; My Son, give me thy heart; God means the whole man. Though the Apostle say, The eye is not the man, nor the ear is not the man, he does not say, The heart is not the man: the heart is the man, the heart is all. And, as Moses was not satisfied with that commission that Pharaoh offered him, that all the young men might go to offer sacrifice, but Moses would have all their young and all their old, all their sons and all their daughters, all their flocks and all their herds, he would have all, so, when God says, *Fili, da mihi Cor*, My Son, give me thy heart, God will not be satisfied with the eye, if I contemplate him in his works (for that's but the godliness of the natural man), nor satisfied with the ear, with hearing many sermons (for that's but a new invention, a new way of making beads, if, as the papist thinks all done if he have said so many *Aves*, I think all done if I have heard so many sermons). But God requires the heart, the whole man, all the faculties of that man: for only that that is entire and indivisible is immoveable; and that that God calls for, and we seek for, in this stem of Pythagoras his symbolical letter, is this immovableness, this fixation of the heart. And yet, even against this, though it be natural, there are many impediments. We shall reduce them to a few, to three, these three. First, there is *Cor nullum*, a mere heartlessness, no heart at all, incogitancy, inconsideration; and then there is *Cor & Cor, Cor duplex*, a double heart, a doubtful, a distracted heart, which is not incogitancy, nor inconsideration, but perplexity and irresolution; and lastly, *Cor vagum*, a wandering, a wayfaring, a weary heart, which is neither inconsideration, nor irresolution, but inconstancy. And this is a trinity against our unity, three enemies to that fixation and entireness of the heart which God loves: inconsideration, when we do not debate; irresolution, when we do not determine; inconstancy, when we do not persevere: and upon each of these, be pleased to stop your devotion a few minutes.

The first is *Cor nullum*, no heart at all, incogitancy, thoughtlessness. An idle body is a disease in a State; an idle soul is a monster in a man. That body that will not work, must not eat, but starve: that soul that does not think, not consider, cannot be said to actuate (which is the proper operation of the soul), but to evaporate; not to work in the body, but to breathe, and smoke through the body. We have seen estates of private men wasted by inconsideration as well as by riot; and a soul may perish by a thoughtlessness as well as by ill thoughts. God takes it as ill to be slighted as to be injured, and God is as much slighted *in Corde nullo*, in our thoughtlessness and inconsideration, as he is opposed and provoked *in Corde maligno*, in a rebellious heart. There is a good nullification of the heart, a good bringing of the heart to nothing, for the fire of God's spirit may take hold of me, and (as the disciples that went with Christ to Emmaeus were affected) my heart may burn within me, when the Scriptures are opened, that is, when God's judgements are denounced against my sin; and this heat may overcome my former frigidity and coldness, and overcome my succeeding tepidity and lukewarmness, and may bring my heart to a mollification, to a tenderness, as Job found it; the Almighty hath troubled me, and made my heart soft; for there are hearts of clay, as well as hearts of wax, hearts whom these fires of God, his corrections, harden. But if these fires of his, these denunciations of his judgements, have overcome first my coldness and then my lukewarmness, and made my heart soft for better impressions, the work is well advanced but it is not all done. For metal may be soft, but not fusil; iron may be red hot, and yet not apt to run into another mould. Therefore there is a liquefaction, a melting, a pouring out of the heart, such as Rahab speaks of to Joshua's spies: As soon as we heard how miraculously God had proceeded in your behalf, in drying up Jordan, all our hearts melted within us, and no man had any spirit left in him. And when upon the consideration of God's miraculous judgements or mercies I come to such a melting and pouring out of my heart that there be no spirit, that is, none of my own spirit left in me; when I have so exhausted, so evacuated myself, that is, all confidence in myself, that I come into the hands of my God, as pliably, as ductily, as that first clod of earth of which he made me in Adam, was in his hands, in which clod of earth, there was no kind of reluctation against God's purpose: this is a blessed nullification of the heart. When I say to myself, as the Apostle professed of himself, *I am nothing*; and then say to God, Lord, though I be nothing, yet behold, I present thee as much as thou hadst to make the whole world of; O Thou that madest the whole world of nothing, make me, that am nothing in mine own eyes, a new creature in Christ Jesus: this is a blessed nullification, a glorious annihilation of the heart. So is there also a blessed nullification thereof in the contrition of the heart, in the sense of my sins; when, as a sharp wind may have worn out a marble statue, or a continual spout worn out a marble pavement, so, my holy tears, made holy in his blood that gives them a tincture, and my holy sighs, made holy in that spirit that breathes them in me, have worn out my marble heart, that is, the marbleness of my heart, and emptied the room of that former heart, and so given God a vacuity, a new place to create a new heart in. But when God hath thus created a new heart, that is, re-enabled me, by his ordinance, to some holy function, then, to put this heart to nothing, to think nothing, to consider nothing; not to know our age, but by the church book, and not by any action done in the course of our lives, for our God, for our prince, for our country, for our neighbour, for ourselves (ourselves are our souls); not to know the seasons of the year but by the fruits which we eat, and not by observation of the public and national blessings which he hath successfully given us; not to know religion, but by the convenience and the preferments to be had in this, or in the other side; to sit here, and not to know if we be asked upon a surprise, whether it were a prayer, or a sermon, or an anthem that we heard last: this is such a nullification of the heart, such an annihilation, such an exinanition thereof, as reflects upon God himself. For, *Respuit datorem, qui datum deserit*, He that makes no use of a benefit despises the benefactor. And therefore, A rod for his back, *qui indiget Corde*, that is without a heart, without consideration what he should do; nay, what he does. For this is the first enemy of this firmness and fixation of the heart, without which we have no treasure. And we have done with that, *Cor nullum*, and pass to the second, *Cor & cor*, *Cor duplex*, the double, the divided, the distracted heart, which is not incon-sideration, but irresolution.

This irresolution, this perplexity is intended in that com-mination from God, The Lord shall give them a trembling heart. This is not that *Cor nullum*, that melted heart, in which There was no spirit left in them, as in Joshua's time; but *Cor pavidum*, a heart that should not know where to settle, nor what to wish; but, as it follows there, In the morning he shall say, Would God it were evening; and in the evening, Would God it were morning. And this is that which Solomon may have in-tended in his prayer, Give thy servant an understanding heart: *Cor Docile*, so St Jerome reads it, a heart able to conceive counsel: for that's a good disposition, but it is not all. For the original is *Leb shemmeany*, that is, *Cor audiens*, a heart willing to hearken to counsel. But all that is not all that is asked; Solomon asks there a heart to discern between good and evil; so that it is a prayer for the spirit of discretion, of conclusion, of resolution; that God would give him a heart willing to receive counsel, and a heart capable to conceive and digest counsel, and a heart able to discern between counsel and counsel, and to resolve, con-clude, determine. It were a strange ambitious patience in any man to be content to be racked every day in hope to be an inch or two taller at last; so it is for me to think to be a dram or two wiser, by hearkening to all jealousies and doubts and distractions and perplexities that arise in my bosom, or in my family, which is the rack and torture of the soul. A spirit of contradiction may be of use in the greatest counsels, because thereby matters may be brought into further debatement. But a spirit of contradiction in mine own bosom, to be able to conclude nothing, resolve nothing, determine nothing, not in my religion, not in my manners, but occasionally, and upon emergencies: this is a sickly complexion of the soul, a dangerous impotency, and a shrewd and ill-presaging *crisis*. If Joshua had suspended his assent of serving the Lord till all his neighbours and their families, all the kings and kingdoms about him, had declared theirs the same way, when would Joshua have come to that protestation: I and my house will serve the Lord? If Esther had forborne to press for an audience to the King, in the behalf and for the life of her nation, till nothing could have been said against it, when would Esther have come to that protestation: I will go; and if I perish, I perish? If one millstone fell from the North Pole, and another from the South, they would meet and they would rest in the centre; Nature would concentre them. Not to be able to concentre those doubts which arise in myself in a resolution at last, whether in moral or in religious actions, is rather a vertiginous giddiness than a wise circumspection or wariness. When God prepared great armies, it is expressed always so: *Tanquam unus vir*, Israel went out, as one man. When God established his beloved David to be king, it is expressed so: *Uno Corde*, he sent them out, with one heart, to make David king. When God accelerated the propagation of his church, it is expressed so: *Una Anima*, The multitude of them that believed were of one heart and one soul. Since God makes nations and armies and churches one heart, let not us make one heart two in ourselves: a divided, a distracted, a perplexed, an irresolved heart; but in all cases, let us be able to say to ourselves, This we should do. God asks the heart, a single heart, an entire heart; for whilst it is so, God may have some hope of it. But when it is a heart and a heart, a heart for God and a heart for Mammon, howsoever it may seem to be even, the odds will be on Mammon's side against God; because he presents possessions, and God but reversions; he the present and possessory things of this world, God but the future and speratory things of the next. So then, the *Cor nullum*, no heart, thoughtlessness, incogitancy, inconsideration, and the *Cor duplex*, the perplexed and irresolved and inconclusive heart, do equally oppose this firmness and fixation of the heart which God loves, and which we consider in this stem and stalk of Pythagoras his symbolic letter. And so does that which we proposed for the third, the *Cor Vagum*, the wandering, the wayfaring, the inconstant heart.

Many times, in our private actions, and in the cribration and sifting of our consciences (for that's the sphere I move in, and no higher), we do overcome the first difficulty, inconsideration: we consider seriously; and sometimes the second, irresolution: we resolve confidently; but never the third, inconstancy: if so far as to bring holy resolutions into actions, yet never so far as to bring holy actions into habits. That word which we read deceitful (The heart is deceitful above all things; who can know it?) is in the original *gnacob*; and that is not only *fraudulentum*, but *versipelle*, deceitful because it varies itself into diverse forms; so that it does not only deceive others (others find not our heart the same towards them today that it was yesterday) but it deceives ourselves; we know not what nor where our heart will be hereafter. Upon those words of Isaiah, *Redite praevaricatores ad Cor*; Return O sinner, to thy heart, *Longe eos mittit*, says St Gregory: God knows whither that sinner is sent that is sent to his own heart, for where is thy heart? Thou mayest remember where it was yesterday: at such an office, at such a chamber; but yesterday's affections are changed today, as today's will be tomorrow. They have despised my judgements; so God complains in Ezekiel; that is, they are not moved with my punishments; they call all, natural accidents, and then it follows: They have polluted my Sabbaths; they are come to a more faint and dilute and indifferent way in their religion. Now what hath occasioned this indifferent way in their religion? Now what hath occasioned this neglecting of God's judgements, and this diluteness and indifference in the ways of religion? That that follows there, Their hearts went after their idols. Went? Whither? Everywhither: for *Quot vitia tot recentes deos*; so many habitual sins, so many idols. And so every man hath some idol, some such sin; and then, that idol sends him to a further idol, that sin to another; for every sin needs the assistance and countenance of another sin, for disguise and palliation. We are not constant in our sins, much less in our more holy purposes. We complain, and justly, of the Church of Rome, that she would not have us receive *in utraque*, in both kinds. But, alas! who amongst us, does receive *in utraque*, so as that when he receives bread and wine, he receives with a true sorrow for former, and a true resolution against future sins? Except the Lord of Heaven create new hearts in us of ourselves we have *Cor Nullum*, no heart; all vanishes into incogitancy. Except the Lord of Heaven concentre our affections, of ourselves, we have *Cor & Cor*, a cloven, a divided heart, a heart of irresolution. Except the Lord of Heaven fix our resolutions, of ourselves, we have *Cor vagum*, a various, a wandering heart; all smokes into inconstancy. And all these three are enemies to that firmness and fixation of the heart which God loves and we seek after. But yet how variously soever the heart do wander, and how little a while soever it stays upon one object, yet, that that thy heart does stay upon, Christ in this place calls thy treasure. For the words admit well that inversion; Where your treasure is, there will your heart be also implies this; where your heart is, that is your treasure. And so we pass from this stem and stalk of Pythagoras his symbolic letter, the firmness and fixation of the heart, to the horns and beams thereof: a broader (but on the left hand), and in that, the corruptible treasures of this world; and a narrower (but on the right hand), and in that, the everlasting treasures of the next. On both sides, that that you fix your heart upon is your treasure: For, where your heart is, there is your treasure also.

Literally, primarily, radically, thesaurus, treasure, is no more but *Depositum in crastinum*, provision for tomorrow; to show how little a proportion, a regulated mind and a contented heart may make a treasure. But we have enlarged the signification of these words, provision and tomorrow: for provision must signify all that can any way be compassed; and tomorrow must signify as long as there shall be a tomorrow, till time shall be no more. But waiving these infinite extensions and perpetuities, is there anything of that nature as (taking the word treasure in the narrowest signification, to be but provision for tomorrow) we are sure shall last till tomorrow? Sits any man here in an assurance that he shall be the same tomorrow that he is now? You have your honours, your offices, your possessions, perchance under seal, a seal of wax, wax that hath a tendency, an adhering, a cleaving nature, to show the royal constancy of his heart that gives them, and would have them continue with you and stick to you. But then, wax, if it be heat, hath a melting, a fluid, a running nature too. So have these honours and offices and possessions to them that grow too hot, too confident in them, or too imperious by them. For these honours and offices and possessions you have a seal, a fair and just evidence of assurance; but have they any seal upon you, any assurance of you till tomorrow? Did our blessed Saviour give day, or any hope of a tomorrow, to that man, to whom he said, Fool, this night they fetch away thy soul? Or is there any of us that can say Christ said not that to him?

But yet a treasure every man hath: An evil man, out of the evil treasure of his heart, bringeth forth that which is evil, says our Saviour: every man hath some sin upon which his heart is set; and, Where your heart is, there is your treasure also. The treasures of wickedness profit nothing, says Job. 'Tis true, but yet treasures of wickedness there are. Are there not yet treasures of wickedness in the house of the wicked? Consider the force of that word, *yet*: *yet* though you have the power of a vigilant prince executed by just magistrates; *yet* though you have the piety of a religious prince, seconded by the assiduity of a laborious clergy; *yet* though you have many helps, which your fathers did, and your neighbours do want, and have (by God's grace) some fruits of those many helps; *yet*, for all this, Are there not yet treasures of wickedness in the house of the wicked? No? Are there not scant measures? which are an abomination to God, says the prophet there; which are not only false measures of merchandise, but false measures of men. For when God says that, he intends all this; is there not yet supplantation in court and misrepresentation of men? When Solomon, who understood subordination of places which flowed from him, as well as the highest, which himself possessed, says, and says experimentally for his own, and prophetically for future times, If a ruler (a man in a great place) hearken to lies, all his servants are wicked, are there not yet misrepresentations of men in courts? Is there not yet oppression in the country? A starving of men and pampering of dogs? A swallowing of the needy? A buying of the poor for a pair of shoes, and a selling to the hungry refuse corn? Is there not yet oppression in the country? Is there not yet extortion in Westminster? A justifying of the wicked for a reward, and a taking away of the righteousness of the righteous from him? Is there not yet extortion in Westminster? Is there not yet collusion and circumvention in the City? Would they not seem richer than they are when they deal in private bargains with one another? And would they not seem poorer than they are when they are called to contribute for the public? Have they not increased their riches by trade, and lifted up their hearts upon the increase of their riches? Have they not slackened their trade, and lain down upon clothes laid to pledge, and ennobled themselves by an ignoble and lazy way of gain? Is there not yet collusion and circumvention in the City? Is there not yet hypocrisy in the Church? In all parts thereof? Half preachings and half hearings? Hearings and preachings without practice? Have we not national sins of our own, and yet exercise the nature of islanders in importing the sins of foreign parts? And though we better no foreign commodity nor manufacture that we bring in, we improve the sins of other nations; and, as a weaker grape, growing upon the Rhine, contracts a stronger nature in the Canaries, so do the sins of other nations transplanted among us. Have we not secular sins, sins of our own age, our own time, and yet sin by precedent of former, as well as create precedents for future? And not only silver and gold, but vessels of iron and brass were brought into the treasury of the Lord; not only the glorious sins of high places, and national sins, and secular sins; but the wretchedest beggar in the street contributes to this treasure, the treasure of sin; and to this mischievous use, to increase this treasure, the treasure of sin, is a subsidy man. He begs in Jesus' name, and for God's sake; and in the same name curses him that does not give. He counterfeits a lameness, or he loves his lameness and would not be cured; for his lameness is his stock, it is his demean, it is (as they call their occupations in the city) his mystery. Are there not yet treasures of wickedness in the house of the wicked, when even they who have no houses, but lie in the streets, have these treasures?

There are. And then, as the nature of treasure is to multiply, so does this treasure, this treasure of sin. It produces another treasure, *Thesaurizamus iram*, we treasure up unto ourselves wrath against the day of wrath: for it is of the sins of the people that God speaks when he says, Is not this laid up in store with me, and sealed up amongst my treasures? He treasures up the sins of the disobedient, but where? In the treasury of his judgements. And then that treasury he opens against us in this world, his treasures of snow and treasures of hail, that is, unseasonableness of weather, barrenness and famine; and he bringeth his winds out of his treasury, contrary winds, or storms and tempests, to disappoint our purposes; and, as he says to Cyrus, I will give thee (even thee *Cyrus*, though God cared not for Cyrus, otherwise than as he had made Cyrus his scourge), I will give thee the treasures of darkness, and the hidden treasures of secret places. God will enable enemies (though he loves not those enemies) to afflict that people that love not him. And these, war and dearth and sickness, are the weapons of God's displeasure; and these he pours out of his treasury, in this world. But then, for the world to come, He shall open his treasury (for whatsoever moved our translators to render that word armoury and not treasury, in that place, yet evidently it is treasury, and in that very word, otzar, which they translate treasury, in all those places of Job and David and Isaiah which we mentioned before, and in all other places), He shall open that treasury (says that prophet) and bring forth the weapons, not as before, of displeasure, but in a far heavier word, the weapons of his indignation. And in the bowels and treasury of his mercy, let me beseech you not to call the denouncing of God's indignation a satyr of a poet, or an invective of an orator. As Solomon says, There is a time for all things; there is a time for consternation of presumptuous hearts, as well as for redintegration of broken hearts; and the time for that is this time of mortification, which we enter into, now. Now therefore, let me have leave to say that the indignation of God is such a thing as a man would be afraid to think he can express it, afraid to think he does know it, for the knowledge of the indignation of God implies the sense and feeling thereof: all knowledge of that is experimental; and that's a woeful way, and a miserable acquisition and purchase of knowledge. To recollect, treasure is provision for the future. No worldly thing is so: there is no certain future, for the things of this world pass from us, we pass from them, the world itself passes away to nothing. Yet a way we have found to make a treasure, a treasure of sin; and we teach God thrift and providence. For when we arm, God arms too; when we make a treasure, God makes a treasure too, a treasure furnished with weapons of displeasure for this world, and weapons of indignation for the world to come. But then, As an evil man, out of the evil treasure of his heart, bringeth forth that which is evil; so (says our Saviour) the good man, out of the good treasure of his heart, bringeth forth that which is good. Which is the last stroke that makes up Pythagoras his symbolical letter, that horn, that beam thereof, which lies on the right hand: a narrower way, but to a better land; through straits, 'tis true, but to the Pacific Sea, the consideration of the treasure of the godly man in this world, and God's treasure towards him, both in this, and the next.

Things dedicated to God are called often The treasures of God; *Thesauri Dei* and *Thesauri sanctorum Dei*. The treasures of God, and the treasures of the servants of God, are, in the Scriptures, the same thing; and so a man may rob God's treasury in robbing a hospital. Now, though to give a talent or to give a jewel or to give a considerable proportion of plate be an addition to a treasury, yet to give a treasury to a treasury is a more precious and a more acceptable present, as to give a library to a library is more than to give the works of any one author. A godly man is a library in himself, a treasury in himself, and therefore fittest to be dedicated and appropriated to God. Invest thyself therefore with this treasure of godliness. What is godliness? Take it in the whole compass thereof, and godliness is nothing but the fear of God. For he that says in his first chapter *Initium sapientae*, The fear of God is the beginning of wisdom, says also in the 22nd *Finis Modiestae*, The fear of God is the end of modesty, the end of humility: no man is bound to direct himself to any lower humiliation than to the fear of God. When God promised good Ezekias all those blessings, wisdom and knowledge and stability and strength of salvation, that that was to defray him and carry him through all was this: The fear of the Lord shall be his treasure. And therefore *Thesaurizate vobis fundamentum*, Lay up in store for yourselves a good foundation against the time to come. Do all in the fear of God: in all warlike preparations, remember the Lord of Hosts, and fear him; in all treaties of peace, remember the Prince of Peace, and fear him; in all consultations, remember the angel of the great council, and fear him. Fear God as much at noon as at midnight, as much in the glory and splendour of His sunshine as in His darkest eclipses. Fear God as much in thy prosperity as in thine adversity, as much in thy preferment as in thy disgrace. Lay up a thousand pound today in comforting that oppressed soul that sues, and lay up ten thousand pound tomorrow in paring his nails that oppresses; lay up a million one day in taking God's cause to heart, and lay up ten millions next day in taking God's cause in hand. Let every soul lay up a penny now in resisting a small temptation, and a shilling anon in resisting a greater. And it will grow to be a treasure, a treasure of talents, of so many talents as that the poorest soul in the congregation would not change treasure with any plate fleet nor *terra firma* fleet nor with those three thousand millions, which (though it be perchance a greater sum than is on the face of Europe, at this day, after a hundred years' embowelling of the earth for treasure) David is said to have left for the treasure of the Temple, only to be laid up in the treasury thereof when it was built; for the charge of the building thereof was otherwise defrayed. Let your conversation be in Heaven. Cannot you get thither? You may see, as St John did, Heaven come down to you. Heaven is here, here in God's Church, in his word, in his sacraments, in his ordinances. Set thy heart upon them, the promises of the Gospel, the seals of reconciliation, and thou hast that treasure which is thy *viaticum* for thy transmigration out of this world, and thy bill of exchange for the world thou goest to. For as the wicked make themselves a treasure of sin and vanity, and then God opens upon them a treasure of his displeasure here and his indignation hereafter, so the godly make themselves a treasure of the fear of God, and he opens unto them a treasure of grace and peace here, and a treasure of joy and glory hereafter. And when of each of these treasures, here and hereafter, I shall have said one word, I have done.

We have treasure, though *in* earthen vessels, say the Apostle. We have; that is, we have already the treasure of grace and peace and faith and justification and sanctification; but yet, in earthen vessels, in vessels that may be broken: peace that may be interrupted, grace that may be resisted, faith that may be enfeebled, justification that may be suspected, and sanctification that may be blemished. But we look for more: for joy and glory, for such a justification and such a sanctification as shall be sealed and riveted in a glorification. Manna putrefied if it were kept by any man but a day; but in the Ark it never putrefied. That treasure which is as manna from Heaven, grace and peace, yet here hath a brackish taste; when grace and peace shall become joy and glory in Heaven, there it will be sincere. *Sordescit quod inferiori miscetur naturae, etsi in suo genere non sordidetur.* Though in the nature thereof that with which a purer metal is mixed be not base, yet it abases the purer metal.

He puts his example in silver and gold: though silver be a precious metal, yet it abases gold. Grace and peace and faith are precious parts of our treasure here. Yet if we mingle them, that is, compare them with the joys and glory of Heaven; if we come to think that our grace and peace and faith here can no more be lost than our joy and glory there, we abase and over-allay those joys and that glory. The kingdom of Heaven is like to a treasure, says our Saviour. But is that all? Is any treasure like unto it? None, for (to end where we began) treasure is *depositum in crastinum*, provision for tomorrow. The treasure of the worldly man is not so; he is not sure of anything tomorrow. Nay, the treasure of the godly man is not so in this world; he is not sure that this day's grace and peace and faith shall be his tomorrow. When I have joy and glory in Heaven, I shall be sure of that, tomorrow. And that's a term long enough, for before a tomorrow there must be a night; and shall there ever be a night in Heaven? No more than day in Hell. There shall be no sun in Heaven; therefore no danger of a sunset. And for the treasure itself, when the Holy Ghost hath told us that the walls and streets of the city are pure gold, that the foundations thereof are all precious stones, and every gate of an entire pearl, what hath the Holy Ghost himself left to denote unto us what the treasure itself within is? The treasure itself is the Holy Ghost himself, and joy in him. As the Holy Ghost proceeds from Father and Son, but I know not how; so there shall something proceed from Father, Son and Holy Ghost, and fall upon me, but I know not what. Nay, not fall upon me neither, but enwrap me, embrace me, for I shall not be below them, so as that I shall not be upon the same seat with the Son, at the right hand of the Father, in the union of the Holy Ghost: rectified by the power of the Father, and feel no weakness; enlightened by the wisdom of the Son, and feel no scruple; established by the joy of the Holy Ghost, and feel no jealousy. Where I shall find the fathers of the first age, dead five thousand years before me; and they shall not be able to say they were there a minute before me. Where I shall find the blessed and glorious martyrs, who went not *per viam lacteum*, but *per viam sanguineam*; not by the milky way of innocent life, but by the bloody way of a violent death; and they shall not contend with me for precedency in their own right, or say, We came in by purchase, and you but by pardon. Where I shall find the virgins, and not be despised by them for not being so; but hear that redintegration, which I shall receive in Christ Jesus, called virginity and entireness. Where all tears shall be wiped from mine eyes, not only tears of compunction for myself and tears of compassion for others but even tears of joy, too: for there shall be no sudden joy, no joy unexperienced there; there I shall have all joys, altogether, always. There Abraham shall not be gladder of his own salvation than of mine, nor I surer of the everlastingness of my God than of my everlastingness in him. This is that treasure of which the God of this treasure give us those spangles; and that single money which this mint can coin, this world can receive, that is, prosperity, and a good use thereof, in worldly things; and grace and peace and faith in spiritual. And then reserve for us the exaltation of this treasure, in the joy and glory of Heaven, in the mediation of His son Christ Jesus, and by the operation of his blessed Spirit.

Amen.

Death's Duel

Or, a consolation to the soul against the dying life and living death of the body

25th February 1631

Delivered in a sermon at Whitehall, before the King's majesty, in the beginning of Lent. Being his last sermon, and called by his Majesty's household, the doctor's own Funeral sermon.

> And unto God the Lord belong the issues of death
> (i.e. from death).
> Psalm 68:20

Buildings stand by the benefit of their foundations that sustain and support them, and of their buttresses that comprehend and embrace them, and of their contignations that knit and unite them. The foundations suffer them not to sink, the buttresses suffer them not to swerve, and the contignation and knitting suffers them not to cleave. The body of our building is in the former part of this verse. It is this: He that is our God is the God of salvation; *ad salutes*, of salvations in the plural, so it is in the original; the God that gives us spiritual and temporal salvation too. But of this building, the foundation, the buttresses, the contignations, are in this part of the verse which constitutes our text, and in the three divers acceptations of the words amongst our expositors: Unto God the Lord belong the issues from death. For first, the foundation of this building (that our God is the God of all salvation) is laid in this, that unto this God the Lord belong the issues of death; that is, it is in his power to give us an issue and deliverance, even then when we are brought to the jaws and teeth of death, and to the lips of that whirlpool, the grave. And so in this acceptation, this *exitus mortis*, this issue of death is *liberatio à morte*, a deliverance from death, and this is the most obvious and most ordinary acceptation of these words, and that upon which our translation lays hold, the issues from death. And then, secondly, the buttresses that comprehend and settle this building, that he that is our God is the God of all salvation, are thus raised; unto God the Lord belong the issues of death, that is, the disposition and manner of our death; what kind of issue and transmigration we shall have out of this world, whether prepared or sudden, whether violent or natural, whether in our perfect senses or shaken and disordered by sickness, there is no condemnation to be argued out of that, no judgement to be made upon that, for, howsoever they die, precious in his sight is the death of his saints, and with him are the issues of death; the ways of our departing out of this life are in his hands. And so in this sense of the words, this *exitus mortis*, the issue of death, is *liberatio in morte*, a deliverance in death. Not that God will deliver us from dying, but that he will have a care of us in the hour of death, of what kind soever our passage be. And in this sense and acceptation of the words, the natural frame and contexture doth well and pregnantly administer unto us. And then, lastly, the contignation and knitting of this building, that he that is our God is the God of all salvations, consists in this, Unto this God the Lord belong the issues of death; that is, that this God the Lord having united and knit both natures in one, and being God, having also come into this world, in our flesh, he could have no other means to save us, he could have no other issue out of this world, nor return to his former glory, but by death. And so in this sense, this *exitus mortis*, this issue of death, is *liberatio per mortem*, a deliverance by death, by the death of this God, our Lord Christ Jesus. And this is Saint Augustine's acceptation of the words, and those many and great persons that have adhered to him. In all these three lines, then, we shall look upon these words. First, as the God of power, the Almighty Father rescues his servants from the jaws of death. And then, as the God of mercy, the glorious Son rescued us, by taking upon himself this issue of death. And then between these two, as the God of comfort, the Holy Ghost rescues us from all discomfort by his blessed impressions beforehand, that what manner of death soever be ordained for us, yet this *exitus mortis* shall be *introitus in vitam*, our issue in death shall be an entrance into everlasting life. And these three considerations: our deliverance *à morte, in morte, per mortem*, from death, in death, and by death, will abundantly do all the offices of the foundations, of the buttresses, of the contignation of this our building. That he that is our God, is the God of all salvation, because unto this God the Lord belong the issues of death.

First, then, we consider this *exitus mortis* to be *liberatio à morte*, that with God the Lord are the issues of death, and therefore in all our deaths, and deadly calamities of this life, we may justly hope of a good issue from him. In all our periods and transitions in this life, are so many passages from death to death. Our very birth and entrance into this life is *exitus à morte*, an issue from death, for in our mother's womb we are dead, so as that we do not know we live, not so much as we do in our sleep, neither is there any grave so close, or so putrid a prison, as the womb would be unto us, if we stayed in it beyond our time, or died there before our time. In the grave the worms do not kill us, we breed and feed, and then kill those worms which we ourselves produced. In the womb the dead child kills the mother that conceived it, and is a murderer, nay, a parricide, even after it is dead. And if we be not dead so in the womb, so as that being dead we kill her that gave us our first life, our life of vegetation, yet we are dead so as David's idols are dead. In the womb we have eyes and see not, ears and hear not. There in the womb we are fitted for works of darkness, all the while deprived of light; and there in the womb we are taught cruelty, by being fed with blood, and may be damned, though we be never born. Of our very making in the womb, David says, I am wonderfully and fearfully made, and such knowledge is too excellent for me, for even that is the Lord's doing, and it is wonderful in our eyes. *Ipse fecit nos*, it is he that hath made us, and not we ourselves, no, nor our parents neither. Thy hands have made and fashioned me round about, saith Job, and (as the original word is) thou hast taken pains about me, and yet (says he) thou dost destroy me. Though I be the masterpiece of the greatest master (man is so), yet if thou do no more for me, if thou leave me where thou madest me, destruction will follow. The womb which should be the house of life, becomes death itself if God leave us there. That which God threatens so often, the shutting of the womb, is not so heavy nor so discomfortable a curse in the first as in the latter shutting, nor in the shutting of barrenness as in the shutting of weakness, when children are come to the birth, and there is not strength to bring forth.

It is the exaltation of misery to fall from a near hope of happiness. And in that vehement imprecation, the prophet expresses the height of God's anger, Give them, O Lord, what will thou give them? give them a miscarrying womb. Therefore as soon as we are men (that is, inanimated, quickened in the womb), though we cannot ourselves, our parents have to say in our behalf: wretched man that he is, who shall deliver him from this body of death? For even the womb is a body of death, if there be no deliverer. It must be he that said to Jeremiah, Before I formed thee I knew thee, and before thou camest out of the womb I sanctified thee. We are not sure that there was no kind of ship nor boat to fish in, nor to pass by, till God prescribed Noah that absolute form of the Ark. That word which the Holy Ghost, by Moses, useth for the Ark, is common to all kind of boats, *Thebah*; and is the same word that Moses useth for the boat that he was exposed in, that his mother laid him in an ark of bulrushes. But we are sure that Eve had no midwife when she was delivered of Cain, therefore she might well say, *Possedi virum à Domino*, I have gotten a man from the Lord, wholly, entirely from the Lord. It is the Lord that enabled me to conceive, the Lord that infused a quickening soul into that conception, the Lord that brought into the world that which himself had quickened; without all this might Eve say, my body had been but the house of death, and *Domini Domini sunt exitus mortis*, to God the Lord belong the issues of death.

But then this *exitus à morte* is but *introitus in mortem*; this issue, this deliverance from that death, the death of the womb, is an entrance, a delivering over to another death, the manifold deaths of this world. We have a winding sheet in our mother's womb which grows with us from our conception, and we come into the world wound up in that winding sheet, for we come to seek a grave. And as prisoners discharged of actions may lie for fees, so when the womb hath discharged us, yet we are bound to it by cords of *hestae*, by such a string as that we cannot go thence, nor stay there; we celebrate our own funerals with cries even at our birth; as though our threescore and ten years of life were spent in our mother's labour, and our circle made up in the first point thereof. We beg one baptism with another, a sacrament of tears; and we come into a world that lasts many ages, but we last not. *In domo patris*, says our Saviour, speaking of heaven, *multae mansiones*, divers and durable, so that if a man cannot possess a martyr's house (he hath shed no blood for Christ), yet he may have a confessor's, he hath been ready to glorify God in the shedding of his blood. And if a woman cannot possess a virgin's house (she hath embraced the holy state of marriage), yet she may have a matron's house, she hath brought forth and brought up children in the fear of God. *In domo patris*, in my Father's house, in heaven, there are many mansions; but here, upon earth the Son of man hath not where to lay his head, saith he himself. *Nonne terram dedit filiis hominum*? How then hath God given this earth to the sons of men? He hath given them earth for their materials to be made of earth, and he hath given them earth for their grave and sepulchre, to return and resolve to earth, but not for their possession. Here we have no continuing city, nay no cottage that continues, nay no persons, no bodies, that continue. Whatsoever moved Saint Jerome to call the journeys of the Israelites in the wilderness, Mansions; the word (the word is *Nasang*) signifies but a journey, but a peregrination. Even the

Israel of God hath no mansions, but journeys, pilgrimages in this life. By what measure did Jacob measure his life to Pharaoh? *The days of the years of my pilgrimage.* And though the apostle would not say *morimur*, that whilst we are in the body we are dead, yet he says, *perigrinamur*, whilst we are in the body we are but in a pilgrimage, and we are absent from the Lord: he might have said dead, for this whole world is but a universal churchyard, but our common grave, and the life and motion that the greatest persons have in it, is but as the shaking of buried bodies in their grave by an earthquake. That which we call life is but *hebdomada mortium*, a week of deaths, seven days, seven periods of our life spent in dying, a dying seven times over; and there is an end. Our birth dies in infancy, and our infancy dies in youth, and youth and the rest die in age, and age also dies and determines all. Nor do all these, youth out of infancy, or age out of youth, arise so, as a phoenix out of the ashes of another phoenix formerly dead, but as a wasp or a serpent out of a carrion, or as a snake out of dung. Our youth is worse than our infancy, and our age worse than our youth. Our youth is hungry and thirsty after those sins which our infancy knew not; and our age is sorry and angry, that it cannot pursue those sins which our youth did. And besides, all the way, so many deaths, that is, so many deadly calamities accompany every condition and every period of this life, as that death itself would be an ease to them that suffer them. Upon this sense doth Job wish that God had not given him an issue from the first death, from the womb: *Wherefore hast thou brought me forth out of the womb? O that I had given up the ghost, and no eye had seen me. I should have been as though I had not been.*

And not only the impatient Israelites in their murmuring (would to God we had died by the hand of the Lord in the land of Egypt), but Elijah himself, when he fled from Jezebel, and went for his life, as that text says, under the juniper tree, requested that he might die, and said, It is enough now, O Lord, take away my life. So Jonah justifies his impatience, nay, his anger, towards God himself: Now, O Lord, take, I beseech thee, my life from me, for it is better for me to die than to live. And when God asked him, Doest thou well to be angry for this, and after (about the gourd), dost thou well to be angry for that, he replies, I do well to be angry, even unto death. How much worse a death than death is this life, which so good men would so often change for death! But if my case be as Saint Paul's case, *quotidiè morior*, that I die daily, that something heavier than death fall upon me every day; if my case be David's case, *tota die mortificamur*; all the day long we are killed, that not only every day, but every hour of the day, something heavier than death fall upon me; though that be true of me, *Conceptus in peccatis*, I was shapen in iniquity, and in sin did my mother conceive me (there I died one death); though that be true of me, *Natus filius irae*, I was born not only the child of sin, but the child of wrath, of the wrath of God for sin, which is a heavier death. Yet *Domini Domini sunt exitus mortis*, with God the Lord are the issues of death; and after a Job, and a Joseph, and a Jeremiah, and a Daniel, I cannot doubt of a deliverance. And if no other deliverance conduce more to his glory and my good, yet he hath the keys of death, and he can let me out at that door, that is, deliver me from the manifold deaths of this world, the *omni die*, and the *tota die*, the everyday's death and every hour's death, by that one death, the final dissolution of body and soul, the end of all.

But then is that the end of all? Is that dissolution of body and soul the last death that the body shall suffer (for of spiritual death we speak not now). It is not. Though this be *exitus à morte*: it is *introitus in mortem*; though it be an issue from the manifold deaths of this world, yet it is an entrance into the death of corruption and putrefaction, and vermiculation, and incineration, and dispersion in and from the grave, in which every dead man dies over again. It was a prerogative peculiar to Christ, not to die this death, not to see corruption. What gave him this privilege? Not Joseph's great proportion of gums and spices, that might have preserved his body from corruption and incineration longer than he needed it, longer than three days, but it would not have done it for ever. What preserved him then? Did his exemption and freedom from original sin preserve him from this corruption and incineration? It is true that original sin hath induced this corruption and incineration upon us; if we had not sinned in Adam, mortality had not put on immortality (as the apostle speaks), nor corruption had not put on incorruption, but we had had our transmigration from this to the other world without any mortality, any corruption at all. But yet since Christ took sin upon him, so far as made him mortal, he had it so far too as might have made him see this corruption and incineration, though he had no original sin in himself. What preserved him then? Did the hypostatical union of both natures, God and man, preserve him from this corruption and incineration? It is true that this was a most powerful embalming, to be embalmed with the divine nature itself, to be embalmed with eternity, was able to preserve him from corruption and incineration for ever. And he was embalmed so, embalmed with the divine nature itself, even in his body as well as in his soul; for the Godhead, the divine nature, did not depart, but remained still united to his dead body in the grave. But yet for all this powerful embalming, his hypostatical union of both natures, we see Christ did die; and for all his union which made him God and man, he became no man (for the union of the body and soul makes the man, and he whose soul and body are separated by death as long as that state lasts, is properly no man). And therefore as in him the dissolution of body and soul was no dissolution of the hypostatical union, so there is nothing that constrains us to say, that though the flesh of Christ had seen corruption and incineration in the grave, this had been any dissolution of the hypostatical union, for the divine nature, the Godhead, might have remained with all the elements and principles of Christ's body, as well as it did with the two constitutive parts of his person, his body and his soul. This incorruption then was not in Joseph's gums and spices, nor was it in Christ's innocency, and exemption from original sin, nor was it (that is, it is not necessary to say it was) in the hypostatical union. But this incorruptibleness of his flesh is most conveniently placed in that; *Non dabis*, thou wilt not suffer thy holy one to see corruption. We look no further for causes or reasons in the mysteries of religion, but to the will and pleasure of God: Christ himself limited his inquisition in that *ita est*, even so, Father, for so it seemed good in thy sight. Christ's body did not see corruption, therefore, because God had decreed it should not. The humble soul (and only the humble soul is the religious soul) rests himself upon God's purposes and his decrees; but then, it is upon those purposes and decrees of God which he hath declared and manifested, not such as are conceived and imagined in ourselves, though upon some probability, some verisimilitude. So, in our present case Peter proceeded in his sermon at Jerusalem, and so Paul in his at Antioch. They preached Christ to have been risen without seeing corruption, not only because God had decreed it, but because he had manifested that decree in his prophet. Therefore doth Saint Paul cite by special number the second Psalm for that decree, and therefore both Saint Peter and Saint Paul cite for it that place in the sixteenth Psalm; for when God declares his decree and purpose in the express words of his prophet, or when he declares it in the real execution of the decree, then he makes it ours, then he manifests it to us. And therefore, as the mysteries of our religion are not the objects of our reason, but by faith we rest on God's decree and purpose (it is so, O God, because it is thy will it should be so) so God's decrees are ever to be considered in the manifestation thereof. All manifestation is either in the word of God, or in the execution of the decree; and when these two concur and meet it is the strongest demonstration that can be: when therefore I find those marks of adoption and spiritual filiation which are delivered in the word of God to be upon me; when I find that real execution of his good purpose upon me, as that actually I do live under the obedience and under the conditions which are evidences of adoption and spiritual filiation; then, and so long as I see these marks and live so, I may safely comfort myself in a holy certitude and a modest infallibility of my adoption. Christ determines himself in that, the purpose of God; because the purpose of God was manifest to him; Saint Peter and Saint Paul determine themselves in those two ways of knowing the purpose of God, the word of God before the execution of the decree in the fullness of time. It was prophesied before, say they, and it is performed now, Christ is risen without seeing corruption.

Now this which is so singularly peculiar to him, that his flesh should not see corruption, at his second coming, his coming to judgement, shall extend to all that are then alive; their flesh shall not see corruption, because (as the apostle says, and says as a secret, as a mystery, Behold I show you a mystery) we shall not all sleep (that is, not continue in the state of the dead in the grave), but we shall all be changed. In an instant we shall have a dissolution, and in the same instant a redintegration, a recompacting of body and soul, and that shall be truly a death and truly a resurrection, but no sleeping, no corruption. But for us that die now and sleep in the state of the dead, we must all pass this *posthume* death, this death after death, nay, this death after burial, this dissolution after dissolution, this death of corruption and putrefaction, of vermiculation and incineration, of dissolution and dispersion in and from the grave. When those bodies that have been the children of royal parents, and the parents of royal children, must say with Job, to Corruption thou art my father, and to the worm, Thou art my mother and my sister. Miserable riddle, when the same worm must be my mother, and my sister and myself! Miserable incest, when I must be married to my mother and my sister, and be both father and mother to my own mother and sister, beget and bear that worm which is all that miserable penury; when my mouth shall be filled with dust, and the worm shall feed, and feed sweetly upon me, when the ambitious man shall have no satisfaction, if the poorest alive tread upon him, nor the poorest receive any contentment in being made equal to princes, for they shall be equal but in dust. One dieth at his full strength, being wholly at ease and in quiet; and another dies in the bitterness of his soul, and never eats with pleasure; but they lie down alike in the dust, and the worm covers them. The worm covers them in Job and in Isaiah, it covers them and is spread under them, the worm is spread under thee, and the worm covers thee. There are the mats and the carpets that lie under, and there are the state and the canopy that hang over the greatest of the sons of men. Even those bodies that were the temples of the Holy Ghost come to this dilapidation, to ruin, to rubbish, to dust; even the Israel of the Lord, and Jacob himself, hath no other specification, no other denomination, but that *vermis Jacob*, thou worm of Jacob. Truly the consideration of this *posthume* death, this death after burial, that after God (with whom are the issues of death) hath delivered me from the death of the womb, by bringing me into the world, and from the manifold deaths of the world, by laying me in the grave, I must die again in an incineration of this flesh, and in a dispersion of that dust. That that monarch, who spread over many nations alive, must in his dust lie in a corner of that sheet of lead, and there but so long as that lead will last; and that private and retired man, that thought himself his own for ever, and never came forth, must in his dust of the grave be published, and (such are the revolutions of the grave) be mingled in his dust with the dust of every highway and of every dunghill, and swallowed in every puddle and pond. This is the most inglorious and contemptible vilification, the most deadly and peremptory nullification of man, that we can consider. God seems to have carried the declaration of his power to a great height, when he sets the prophet Ezekiel in the valley of dry bones, and says, Son of man, can these bones live? as though it had been impossible, and yet they did. The Lord laid sinews upon them, and flesh, and breathed into them, and they did live. But in that case there were

73

bones to be seen, something visible, of which it might be said, Can this thing live? But in this death of incineration and dispersion of dust, we see nothing that we can call that man's. If we say, Can this dust live? Perchance it cannot; it may be the mere dust of the earth, which never did live, nor never shall. It may be the dust of that man's worm, which did live, but shall no more. It may be the dust of another man, that concerns not him of whom it was asked. This death of incineration and dispersion is, to natural reason, the most irrecoverable death of all; and yet *Domini Domini sunt exitus mortis*, unto God the Lord belong the issues of death; and by recompacting this dust into the same body, and reanimating the same body with the same soul, he shall in a blessed and glorious resurrection give me such an issue from this death as shall never pass into any other death, but establish me into a life that shall last as long as the Lord of Life himself.

And so have you that that belongs to the first acceptation of these words (unto God the Lord belong the issues of death). That though from the womb to the grave, and in the grave itself, we pass from death to death, yet, as Daniel speaks, the Lord our God is able to deliver us, and he will deliver us.

And so we pass unto our second accommodation of these words (unto God the Lord belong the issues of death); that it belongs to God, and not to man, to pass a judgement upon us at our death, or to conclude a dereliction on God's part upon the manner thereof.

Those indications which the physicians receive, and those presagitions which they give for death or recovery in the patient, they receive and they give out of the grounds and the rules of their art, but we have no such rule or art to give a presagition of spiritual death and damnation upon any such indication as we see in any dying man; we see often enough to be sorry, but not to despair; for the mercies of God work momentarily in minutes, and many times insensibly to bystanders or any other than the party departing, and we may be deceived both ways: we use to comfort ourselves in the death of a friend, if it be testified that he went away like a lamb, that is, without any reluctation. But God knows that may be accompanied with a dangerous damp and stupefaction, and insensibility of his present state. Our blessed Saviour suffered colluctations with death, and a sadness even in his soul to death, and an agony even to a bloody sweat in his body, and expostulations with God, and exclamations upon the cross. He was a devout man who said upon his death-bed, or death-turf (for he was a hermit), *Septuaginta annos Domino servivisti, et mori times?* Hast thou served a good master threescore and ten years, and now art thou loth to go into his presence? Yet Hilarion was loth. He was a devout man (a hermit too) that said that day he died, *Cogita te hodie caepisse servire Domino, et hodie finiturum*, Consider this to be the first day's service that ever thou didst thy Master, to glorify him in a Christianly and a constant death, and if thy first day be thy last day too, how soon dost thou come to receive thy wages! Yet Barlaam could have been content to have stayed longer for it. Make no ill conclusions upon any man's lothness to die. And then, upon violent deaths inflicted as upon malefactors, Christ himself hath forbidden us by his own death to make any ill conclusion; for his own death had those impressions in it; he was reputed, he was executed as a malefactor, and no doubt many of them who concurred to his death did believe him to be so. Of sudden death there are scarce examples be found in the Scriptures upon good men, for death in battle cannot be called sudden death; but God governs not by examples but by rules, and therefore make no ill conclusion upon sudden death nor upon distempers neither, though perchance accompanied with some words of diffidence and distrust in the mercies of God. The tree lies as it falls, it is true, but it is not the last stroke that fells the tree, nor the last word nor gasp that qualifies the soul. Still pray we for a peaceable life against violent death, and for time of repentance against sudden death, and for sober and modest assurance against distempered and diffident death, but never make ill conclusions upon persons overtaken with such deaths; *Domini Domini sunt exitus mortis*, to God the Lord belong the issues of death. And he received Samson, who went out of this world in such a manner (consider it actively, consider it passively in his own death, and in those whom he slew with himself) as was subject to interpretation hard enough. Yet the Holy Ghost hath moved Saint Paul to celebrate Samson in his great catalogue, and so doth all the church. Our critical day is not the very day of our death, but the whole course of our life. I thank him that prays for me when the bell tolls, but I thank him much more that catechises me, or preaches to me, or instructs me how to live. *Fac hoc et vives*, there is my security, the mouth of the Lord hath said it, do this and thou shalt live. But though I do it, yet I shall die too, die a bodily, a natural death. But God never mentions, never seems to consider that death, the bodily, the natural death. God doth not say, Live well, and thou shalt die well, that is, an easy, a quiet death; but, live well here, and thou shalt live well for ever. As the first part of a sentence pieces well with the last, and never respects, never hearkens after the parenthesis that comes between, so doth a good life here flow into an eternal life, without any consideration what manner of death we die. But whether the gate of my prison be opened with an oiled key (by a gentle and preparing sickness), or the gate be hewn down by a violent death, or the gate be burnt down by a raging and frantic fever, a gate into heaven I shall have, for from the Lord is the cause of my life, and with God the Lord are the issues of death. And further we carry not this second acceptation of the words, as this issue of death is *liberatio in morte*, God's care that the soul be safe, what agonies soever the body suffers in the hour of death. But pass to our third part and last part; as this issue of death is *liberatio per mortem*, a deliverance by the death of another by the death of Christ.

Sufferentiam Job audiisti, et vidisti finem Domini, says Saint James (5:11). You have heard of the patience of Job, says he: all this while you have done that, for in every man, calamitous, miserable man, a Job speaks. Now, see the end of the Lord, sayeth that apostle, which is not that end that the Lord proposed to himself (salvation to us), nor the end which he proposes to us (conformity to him), but see the end of the Lord, says he, the end that the Lord himself came to, death, and a painful and a shameful death. But why did he die? and why die so? *Quia Domini Domini sunt exitus mortis* (as Saint Augustine, interpreting this text, answers that question), because to this God our Lord belonged the issues of death. *Quid apertius diceretur?* says he there, what can be more obvious, more manifest than this sense of these words? In the former part of this verse it is said, He that is our God is the God of salvation; *Deus salvos faciendi*, so he reads it, the God that must save us. Who can that be, says he, but Jesus? For therefore that name was given him because he was to save us. And to this Jesus, says he, this Saviour, belongs the issues of death; *Nec oportuit eum de hac vita alios exitus habere quam mortis.* Being come into this life in our mortal nature, he could not go out of it any other way than by death. *Ideo dictum*, says he, therefore it is said, to God the Lord belong the issues of death; *ut ostenderetur moriendo nos salvos facturum*, to show that his way to save us was to die. And from this text doth Saint Isidore prove that Christ was truly man (which as many sects of heretics denied, as that he was truly God), because to him, though he were *Dominus Dominus* (as the text doubles it), God the Lord, yet to him, to God the Lord belonged the issues of death. *Oportuit eum pati*; more cannot be said than Christ himself says of himself; These things Christ ought to suffer; he had no other way but by death. So then this part of our sermon must needs be a passion sermon, since all his life was a continual passion, all our Lent may well be a continual Good Friday. Christ's painful life took off none of the pains of his death, he felt not the less then for having felt so much before. Nor will any thing that shall be said before, lessen, but rather enlarge your devotion, to that which shall be said of his passion at the time of due solemnization thereof. Christ bled not a drop the less at the last, for having bled at his circumcision before, nor will you shed a tear the less then, if you shed some now. And therefore be now content to consider with me how to this God the Lord belonged the issues of death.

That God, this Lord, the Lord of life, could die, is a strange contemplation; that the Red Sea could be dry, that the sun could stand still, that an oven could be seven times heat and not burn, that lions could be hungry and not bite, is strange, miraculously strange, but super-miraculous that God could die; but that God would die is an exaltation of that. But even of that also it is a super-exaltation, that God should die, must die, and *non exitus* (said Saint Augustine), God the Lord had no issue but by death, and *oportuit pati* (says Christ himself), all this Christ ought to suffer, was bound to suffer; *Deus ultionum Deus*, says David, God is the God of revenges, he would not pass over the sin of man unrevenged, unpunished. But then *Deus ultionum libère egit* (says that place), the God of revenges works freely, he punishes, he spares whom he will. And would he not spare himself? he would not: *Dilectio fortis ut mors*, love is strong as death; stronger, it drew in death, that naturally is not welcome. *Si possibile*, says Christ, if it be possible, let this cup pass, when his love, expressed in a former decree with his Father, had made it impossible. Many waters quench not love. Christ tried many: he was baptised out of his love, and his love determined not there; he wept over Jerusalem out of his love, and his love determined not there. He mingled blood with water in his agony, and that determined not his love; he wept pure blood, all his blood at all his eyes, at all his pores, in his flagellation and thorns (to the Lord our God belonged the issues of blood), and these expressed, but these did not quench his love.

He would not spare, nay, he could not spare himself. There was nothing more free, more voluntary, more spontaneous than the death of Christ. It is true, *libère egit*, he died voluntarily; but yet when we consider the contract that had passed between his Father and him, there was an *oportuit*, a kind of necessity upon him: all this Christ ought to suffer. And when shall we date this obligation, this *oportuit*, this necessity? When shall we say that began? Certainly this decree by which Christ was to suffer all this was an eternal decree, and was there anything before that, that was eternal? Infinite love, eternal love; be pleased to follow this home, and to consider it seriously, that what liberty soever we can conceive in Christ to die or not to die; this necessity of dying, this decree is as eternal as that liberty; and yet how small a matter made he of this necessity and this dying? His Father calls it but a bruise, and but a bruising of his heel (the serpent shall bruise his heel), and yet that was, that the serpent should practise and compass his death. Himself calls it but a baptism, as though he were to be the better for it. I have a baptism to be baptized with, and he was in pain till it was accomplished, and yet this baptism was his death. The Holy Ghost calls it joy (for the joy which was set before him he endured the cross), which was not a joy of his reward after his passion, but a joy that filled him even in the midst of those torments, and arose from them. When Christ calls his passion *Calicem*, a cup, and no worse (Can ye drink of my cup?), he speaks not odiously, not with detestation of it. Indeed it was a cup, *salus mundo*, a health to all the world. And *quid retribuam*, says David, What shall I render to the Lord? Answer you with David, *Accipiam calicem*, I will take the cup of salvation; take it, that cup of salvation, his passion, if not into your present imitation, yet into your present contemplation. And behold how that Lord that was God, yet could die, would die, must die for your salvation.

That Moses and Elias talked with Christ in the transfiguration, both Saint Matthew and Saint Mark tells us, but what they talked of, only Saint Luke; *Dicebant excessum ejus*, says he, They talked of his decease, of his death, which was to be accomplished at Jerusalem. The word is of his exodus, the very word of our text, *exitus*, his issue by death. Moses, who in his exodus had prefigured this issue of our Lord, and in passing Israel out of Egypt through the Red Sea, had foretold in that

79

actual prophecy, Christ's passing of mankind through the sea of his blood; and Elias, whose exodus and issue of this world was a figure of Christ's ascension; had no doubt a great satisfaction in talking with our blessed Lord, *de excessu ejus*, of the full consummation of all this in his death, which was to be accomplished at Jerusalem. Our meditation of his death should be more visceral, and affect us more, because it is of a thing already done. The ancient Romans had a certain tenderness and detestation of the name of death; they could not name death, no, not in their wills. There they could not say, *Si mori contigerit, but si quid humanitas contingat*, not if or when I die, but when the course of nature is accomplished upon me. To us that speak daily of the death of Christ (he was crucified, dead, and buried), can the memory or the mention of our own death be irksome or bitter? There are in these latter times amongst us that name death freely enough, and the death of God, but in blasphemous oaths and execrations. Miserable men, who shall therefore be said never to have named Jesus, because they have named him too often; and therefore hear Jesus say, *Nescivi vos*, I never knew you, because they made themselves too familiar with him. Moses and Elias talked with Christ of his death only in a holy and joyful sense, of the benefit which they and all the world were to receive by that. Discourses of religion should not be out of curiosity, but to edification. And then they talked with Christ of his death at that time when he was in the greatest height of glory, that ever he admitted in this world, that is, his transfiguration. And we are afraid to speak to the great men of this world of their death, but nourish in them a vain imagination of immortality and immutability. But *bonum est nobis esse hic* (as Saint Peter said there), It is good to dwell here, in this consideration of his death, and therefore transfer we our tabernacle (our devotions) through some of those steps which God the Lord made to his issue of death that day.

Take in the whole day from the hour that Christ received the passover upon Thursday unto the hour in which he died the next day. Make this present day that day in thy devotion, and consider what he did, and remember what you have done. Before he instituted and celebrated the sacrament (which was after the eating of the passover), he proceeded to that act of humility, to wash his disciples' feet, even Peter's, who for a while resisted him. In thy preparation to the holy and blessed sacrament, hast thou with a sincere humility sought a reconciliation with all the world, even with those that have been averse from it, and refused that reconciliation from thee? If so (and not else) thou hast spent that first part of this his last day in a conformity with him. After the sacrament he spent the time till night in prayer, in preaching, in psalms: hast thou considered that a worthy receiving of the sacrament consists in a continuation of holiness after, as well as in a preparation before? If so, thou hast therein also conformed thyself to him; so Christ spent his time till night. At night he went into the garden to pray, and he prayed *prolixius*, he spent much time in prayer. How much? Because it is literally expressed, that he prayed there three several times, and that returning to his disciples after his first prayer, and finding them asleep, said, Could ye not watch with me one hour, it is collected that he spent three hours in prayer. I dare scarce ask thee whither thou wentest, or how thou disposedst of thyself, when it grew dark and after last night. If that time were spent in a holy recommendation of thyself to God, and a submission of thy will to his, it was spent in a conformity to him. In that time, and in those prayers, was his agony and bloody sweat. I will hope that thou didst pray; but not every ordinary and customary prayer, but prayer actually accompanied with shedding of tears and dispositively in a readiness to shed blood for his glory in necessary cases, puts thee into a conformity with him. About midnight he was taken and bound with a kiss, art thou not too conformable to him in that? Is not that too literally, too exactly thy case, at midnight to have been taken and bound with a kiss? From thence he was carried back to Jerusalem, first to Annas, then to Caiaphas, and (as late as it was) then he was examined and buffered, and delivered over to the custody of those officers from whom he received all those irrisions, and violences, the covering of his face, the spitting upon his face, the blasphemies of words, and the smartness of blows, which that gospel mentions: in which compass fell that *gallicinium*, that crowing of the cock which called up Peter to his repentance. How thou passedst all that time last night, thou knowest. If thou didst anything that needed Peter's tears, and hast not shed them, let me be thy cock, do it now. Now, thy Master (in the unworthiest of his servants) looks back upon thee, do it now. Betimes, in the morning, so soon as it was day, the Jews held a council in the high priest's hall, and agreed upon their evidence against him, and then carried him to Pilate, who was to be his judge. Didst thou accuse thyself when thou wakedst this morning, and wast thou content to admit even false accusations, that is, rather to suspect actions to have been sin, which were not, than to smother and justify such as were truly sins? Then thou spentest that hour in conformity to him. Pilate found no evidence against him, and therefore to ease himself, and to pass a compliment upon Herod, tetrarch of Galilee, who was at that time at Jerusalem (because Christ, being a Galilean, was of Herod's jurisdiction), Pilate sent him to Herod, and rather as a madman than a malefactor; Herod remanded him (with scorn) to Pilate, to proceed against him; and this was about eight of the clock. Hast thou been content to come to this inquisition, this examination, this agitation, this cribration, this pursuit of thy conscience; to sift it, to follow it from the sins of thy youth to thy present sins, from the sins of thy bed to the sins of thy board, and from the substance to the circumstance of thy sins? That is time spent like thy Saviour's. Pilate would have saved Christ, by using the privilege of the day in his behalf, because that day one prisoner was to be delivered, but they choose Barabbas; he would have saved him from death, by satisfying their fury with inflicting other torments upon him, scourging and crowning with thorns, and loading him with many scornful and ignominious contumelies. But this redeemed him not, they pressed a crucifying. Hast thou gone about to redeem thy sin, by fasting, by alms, by disciplines and mortifications, in the way of satisfaction to the justice of God? That will not serve, that is not the right way; we press an utter crucifying of that sin that governs thee: and that conforms thee to Christ. Towards noon Pilate gave judgement, and they made such haste to execution as that by noon he was upon the cross. There now hangs that sacred body upon the cross, rebaptized in his own tears, and sweat, and embalmed in his own blood alive. There are those bowels of compassion which are so conspicuous, so manifested, as that you may see them through his wounds. There those glorious eyes grew faint in their light, so as the sun, ashamed to survive them, departed with his light too. And then that Son of God, who was never from us, and yet had now come a new way unto us in assuming our nature, delivers that soul (which was never out of his Father's hands) by a new way, a voluntary emission of it into his Father's hands; for though to this God our Lord belonged these issues of death, so that considered in his own contract, he must necessarily die, yet at no breach or battery which they had made upon his sacred body issued his soul; but *emisit*, he gave up the ghost; and as God breathed a soul into the first Adam, so this second Adam breathed his soul into God, into the hands of God.

There we leave you in that blessed dependency, to hang upon him that hangs upon the cross, there bathe in his tears, there suck at his wounds, and lie down in peace in his grave, till he vouchsafe you a resurrection, and an ascension into that kingdom, which he hath purchased for you with the inestimable price of his incorruptible blood.

Amen.

Notes

1. 'Who learned medicine from Cheiron' (Latin).
2. The Chaldee Paraphrase was an Aramaic translation or paraphrase of a portion of the Old Testament.
3. 'From faith' (Latin).
4. 'I shall not die, I shall not die' (Latin).
5. 'Stare' is an old word for starling, from the Latin *sturnus*.

Biographical note

John Donne was born in Bread Street, London, in 1572, the third of six children in an affluent Roman Catholic family. Donne's father was an ironmonger and his mother the great niece of Sir Thomas More. His early life was shadowed by both the peril faced by Catholics during the reign of Elizabeth I, and by death: his father and three of his sisters dying while he was still a child.

Having been educated by Jesuits, Donne attended the universities of Oxford and Cambridge, but was not granted a degree by either as a result of his refusal to take the Oath of Supremacy, which ran counter to his Catholic beliefs. Progressing to study at the London Courts of Law, he spent much of his considerable inheritance in the pursuit of women, literature and travel. It was in 1593, when his brother was imprisoned and later died in prison for the offence of harbouring a Catholic priest, that he began to question his faith.

At the age of 25 he gained esteemed employment in the establishment of Lord Thomas Egerton, but was disgraced and imprisoned when he married, in secret, Egerton's teenage niece Anne More. On their release from prison, the couple were forced to live a secluded life in Pryrford, Surrey, where they and their children were supported by Anne's cousin, and by Donne's paltry wage as a lawyer. Of the couple's eleven children, two were stillborn and a further two died in infancy. Donne was later elected as a Member of Parliament, but Parliamentary employment still being unpaid at this time, he subsisted largely on the income gained by writing poetry for wealthy friends.

In 1615, at King James I's prompting, Donne was ordained into the Church of England, having some years previously expressed dissatisfaction with the Catholic Church in his poetry. Following some time spent in Germany, he rose through the ranks of the Church of England to become Dean of St Paul's in

1621; he retained this position until his death in 1631. The death first of his wife in 1617 and later of his daughter Lucy, in addition to the deaths of close family members which had punctuated his entire life, had a profound effect on the poetry of his later life: although he began his writing career as a satirist and a metaphysical poet of often erotic poetry, his sermons and late poetry are known for their elegiac and mournful beauty.

HESPERUS PRESS

Hesperus Press, as suggested by the Latin motto, is committed to bringing near what is far – far both in space and time. Works written by the greatest authors, and unjustly neglected or simply little known in the English-speaking world, are made accessible through new translations and a completely fresh editorial approach. Through these classic works, the reader is introduced to the greatest writers from all times and all cultures.

For more information on Hesperus Press, please visit our website: **www.hesperuspress.com**

ET REMOTISSIMA PROPE

SELECTED TITLES FROM HESPERUS PRESS

'on'

Author	Title	Foreword writer
William Hazlitt	*On the Elgin Marbles*	Tom Paulin
John Stuart Mill	*On the Subjection of Women*	Fay Weldon

Classics, Modern Voices and Brief Lives

Author	Title	Foreword writer
Cyrano de Bergerac	*Journey to the Moon*	Andrew Smith
Richard Canning	*Brief Lives: Wilde*	
Joseph Conrad	*Heart of Darkness*	A.N. Wilson
Charles Dickens	*Doctor Marigold's Prescriptions*	Gwyneth Lewis
Annie Dillard	*The Maytrees*	
Beppe Fenoglio	*A Private Affair*	Paul Bailey
Yasmine Ghata	*The Calligraphers' Night*	
Johann Wolfgang von Goethe	*The Man of Fifty*	A.S. Byatt
Mikhail Kuzmin	*Wings*	Paul Bailey
Mikhail Lermontov	*A Hero of Our Time*	Doris Lessing
Carlo Levi	*Essays on India*	Anita Desai
Klaus Mann	*Alexander*	Jean Cocteau
Patrick Miles	*Brief Lives: Chekhov*	
Henry Miller	*Aller Retour New York*	
Luigi Pirandello	*The Turn*	
Marquis de Sade	*Betrayal*	John Burnside
Sándor Petőfi	*John the Valiant*	George Szirtes
Leo Tolstoy	*Hadji Murat*	Colm Tóibín